Program Evaluatio1
School Counseling

Program Evaluation in School Counseling is the first book on program evaluation that looks to the field and literature of program evaluation and then relates methods, procedures, and practices back to the practice of school counseling.

Written by two accomplished authors who teamed up to build evaluation capacity among school and school-based counselors internationally, the book highlights their interdisciplinary work, covering many years and several continents. Based on the authors' model for teaching program evaluation and their research on school counselor competence in program evaluation, this concise, clear, and practical guide supports the continuing professional development of school counselors through training, workshops, and self-study. This book addresses the program evaluation knowledge, skills, and understandings that school-based counselors are expected to use in line with the CACREP 2016 Standards.

The book is intended as a companion text for university courses in research methods and/or in the organization and administration of counseling services. It is also appropriate as a self-study guide to help practicing school counselors develop expertise in evaluation.

Michael S. Trevisan, PhD, is dean of the college of education at Washington State University and professor of educational psychology. He has worked in evaluation for 30+ years and is widely published in the field. He has provided numerous evaluation workshops to school counselors in the US and internationally.

John C. Carey, PhD, is an emeritus professor of school counseling and the associate director of the Ronald H. Fredrickson Center for School Counseling Outcomes Research at the University of Massachusetts. He is a leader in evidence-based school counseling and has published extensively. He has offered evaluation training for counselors in Africa, Asia, Europe, Central America, and North America.

Program Evaluation in School Counseling

Improving Comprehensive and
Developmental Programs

Michael S. Trevisan
John C. Carey

Routledge
Taylor & Francis Group

NEW YORK AND LONDON

First published 2020
by Routledge
52 Vanderbilt Avenue, New York, NY 10017

and by Routledge
2 Park Square, Milton Park, Abingdon, Oxon OX14 4RN

Routledge is an imprint of the Taylor & Francis Group, an informa business

© 2020 Taylor & Francis

Library of Congress Cataloging-in-Publication Data
Names: Trevisan, Michael S., author. | Carey, John C., author.
Title: Program evaluation in school counseling : improving
    comprehensive and developmental programs / Michael S. Trevisan
    and John C. Carey.
Description: New York, NY : Routledge, 2020. | Includes
    bibliographical references and index. |
Identifiers: LCCN 2019052631 (print) | LCCN 2019052632
    (ebook) | ISBN 9781138346574 (hardback) | ISBN
    9781138346611 (paperback) | ISBN 9780429437229 (ebook)
Subjects: LCSH: Educational counseling--United States--Evaluation. |
    Evaluation research (Social action programs)--United States.
Classification: LCC LB1027.5 .T72 2020 (print) | LCC LB1027.5
    (ebook) | DDC 371.4--dc23
LC record available at https://lccn.loc.gov/2019052631
LC ebook record available at https://lccn.loc.gov/2019052632

ISBN: 978-1-138-34657-4 (hbk)
ISBN: 978-1-138-34661-1 (pbk)
ISBN: 978-0-429-43722-9 (ebk)

Typeset in Bembo
by Nova Techset Private Limited, Bengaluru & Chennai, India

Contents

Preface

Program Evaluation in School Counseling: Improving Comprehensive and Developmental Programs is a book about how to evaluate school counseling programs. It was written as a practical guide for school counselors in training and for practicing professionals who need to evaluate their work.

Evaluating the comprehensive developmental school counseling program and its constituent services and activities has long been considered an essential part of the work of school counselors. The information gained from evaluation helps us improve the outcomes of our work and demonstrate its value to stakeholders and decision-makers. The American School Counseling Association (ASCA) National Model includes a major program evaluation focus in its accountability section. This book helps school counselors design and implement evaluations that align with the current ASCA National Model. It also helps school counselors design evaluations that address needs that are currently underrepresented in the ASCA National Model. These include the lack of emphasis on formative evaluation that can be used to improve program services and the use of qualitative data and methods that can provide rich, in-depth understanding of various program phenomena.

Unfortunately, for a number of reasons, many school counselors do not engage in program evaluation, despite the recognition of its importance. Many school counselors do not get adequate pre-service or professional development training in conducting program evaluation. Program evaluation is seldom taught as a freestanding course and is most often included as a component of a course in research or a course in the organization and administration of school counseling services. Practical professional development materials on the methods of evaluating school counseling programs do not exist. This book is designed to fill the void of practical training materials for school counseling program evaluation.

This book was inspired by our desire to bring together the fields of evaluation and school counseling which have been estranged for many years. Much of the thinking and terminology around current practices of school counseling program evaluation have been elaborated without the benefit of a connection to exciting developments in the field of evaluation. Conversely, the field of evaluation lacks access to school counseling as important context to apply and test models and approaches. This book provides details for comprehensive, practical program evaluation that looks outward to the field and literature of program evaluation and then relates program evaluation methods, procedures, and practices back to the practice of school counseling.

In *Program Evaluation in School Counseling: Improving Comprehensive and Developmental Programs*, we address current school counseling evaluation practices (e.g., those advocated by the ASCA National Model) and show how these practices can be improved through their connection to the concepts and methods from the field of evaluation. Readers of this book will come away with both skill in current school counseling evaluation practices and also the ability to implement practices that are effective in generating information to improve practices and demonstrate their value.

Who This Book is For

The book was written for a number of potential users in or related to the school counseling profession. It can be used as an instructional text for graduate courses in school counseling programs, a book to support professional development, or a reference for policymakers or school district administrators responsible for school counseling programs. Here is a subset of possible users of this book and reasons why the book would be of benefit:

Faculty and Students will find the book useful in a research methods course or in a course on the organization and administration of school counseling services, courses where program evaluation is typically addressed in pre-service school counseling programs. The book could also support graduate seminars on program evaluation in school counseling. The book is intended to help readers learn practical skills in evaluation and assumes that readers either have or are in the process of acquiring competence through coursework in research methods, and in organization and administration of school counseling programs.

School Counseling Professionals will find the book as an easy-to-understand resource to support the evaluation of their school counseling program. The book could also be a professional development resource, supporting school counselors in professional learning communities.

School Administrators will see this book as a resource for supporting school counselors conducting evaluation of their school counseling program and services. The book will also help administrators to think about and conceptualize a district-wide school counseling evaluation.

State School Counseling Directors will find the book beneficial for helping them see more clearly the role program evaluation can play in support of better services and outcomes for school counseling programs. The book could help them articulate to policymakers what good program evaluation looks like for school counselors and help shape supportive state policies.

How This Book is Organized

This book is organized to provide you with the things you'll need to know and understand about evaluation in order to effectively carry out the evaluation tasks and activities to support your school counseling program. Chapter 1 develops a conceptual understanding of program evaluation for school counselors and introduces the school counseling evaluation framework. Chapter 2 connects evaluation with the school counseling profession more directly by detailing ASCA National Model expectations for program evaluation by school counselors. Chapter 2 grounds evaluation in the context of the school counseling profession, and does so with an eye toward professional practice.

Chapters 3 through 9 are devoted to the school counseling evaluation framework, with each chapter addressing one of the components. Chapter 3 is the first component of the school counseling evaluation framework and focuses on stakeholders in the school counseling program. This chapter will help you identify key stakeholder groups, the importance of including stakeholders in the evaluation process, and ways to do so. Involving culturally diverse stakeholder groups with the idea of implementing a culturally responsive evaluation is a key component of this chapter.

Building off of the importance of stakeholders in program evaluation, Chapter 4 introduces theories of action and logic models as the starting point and central feature of school counseling program evaluation. Logic models represent the "theory" of how the program is assembled to obtain outcomes for students. The basic elements, ways to construct logic models, and key benefits of the use of logic models are provided.

Chapter 5 addresses the importance of and ways to develop evaluation questions. Evaluation questions signal information needs about a program and the kinds of data that will be needed to answer the evaluation questions. The way the evaluation questions are developed, coupled with the features of the program they address, has direct implications for use by school counselors and other stakeholders. This chapter explicitly recognizes this fact, and draws a strong connection to evaluation use, addressed in Chapter 9.

Chapters 6, 7, and 8 address evaluation designs, quantitative methods, and qualitative methods, respectively. Evaluation design and methods have a direct relationship to data analysis, and as such, think of Chapters 6 through 8 as a package within the school counseling evaluation framework chapters.

Communicating and reporting evaluation findings are essential activities for using the evaluation. Chapter 9 addresses evaluation use by providing school counselors with a variety of strategies for communicating and reporting evaluation findings. Addressing stakeholder communication and information needs is a central tenant of Chapter 9.

Chapter 10 provides competencies in evaluation that are important for the professional practice of school counseling. These include field-specific, technical, and nontechnical competencies. In addition, recommendations for navigating the organizational complexities of schools and school districts in order to implement an effective evaluation of the school counseling program are provided. This chapter provides the basis to help you self-assess your professional school counseling competencies in evaluation and identify future evaluation professional development activities.

Additional Features

There are additional features that are unique to Chapters 3 through 9, the school counseling evaluation framework chapters. These features will help you develop further knowledge and understanding about effective evaluation work by school counselors. The first feature consists of vignettes that illustrate best practice with respect to the particular component. For example, since Chapter 4 deals with logic models, a vignette describing well thought practice among school counselors with respect to logic models is provided.

A second feature contained in the book, specifically in Chapters 3 through 9, is the incorporation of accountability features from the ASCA National Model. The ASCA National Model accountability features form the basis for the evaluation ideas and processes that are organized and articulated through the school counseling evaluation framework. In this way, the book supports and builds on the ASCA National Model by looking outward to the field of evaluation and bringing these ideas back to school counseling practice. Note that at the time of the completion of this book, the fourth edition of the ASCA National Model was released (ASCA, 2019). We have reviewed the fourth edition materials and listened to the online ASCA webinars. We conclude that despite revisions to some labels for clarity, and the combining of some forms to streamline, the essential program evaluation features of the ASCA National Model found in the third edition are also present in the fourth edition. There is little in the way of a substantive change in evaluation requirements and procedures in the fourth edition. Thus, the ASCA (2012) references in this book will hold the reader in good stead as they consider and work toward ASCA National Model requirements specified in ASCA (2019).

Third, the Joint Committee on Standards in Education Evaluation (JCSEE) Program Evaluation Standards are woven into the school counseling evaluation framework (Chapters 3 through 9). The JCSEE Program Evaluation Standards represent the best thinking about conducting high-quality evaluation work. Each of the component chapters addresses the most applicable standards in doing school counseling evaluation work, and does so in a way that helps develop what quality evaluation of a school counseling program looks like.

Fourth, the evaluation framework chapters address culturally responsive evaluation. There is strong awareness in the evaluation profession of the importance of doing multiculturally valid evaluation work. These chapters provide strategies and recommendations for developing and carrying out culturally responsive school counseling evaluation.

A glossary follows Chapter 10 which provides a useful reference for terms and concepts used in evaluation. The glossary is listed in alphabetical order with easy-to-read definitions that will prove helpful to the busy school counseling professional. Know that for most terms, the definitions are based on current thinking within the evaluation field. Where differences between school counseling and evaluation are important to address, the definitions provide further clarification.

Final Words

In writing this book, we hope to honor the critically important work that school counselors do to support the academic development and well-being of children and youth. We know that high-quality program evaluation contributes to this work by improving services and demonstrating that the work of counselors has worth and value. We are confident that the application of the evaluation concepts, approaches, and skills in this book will enable school counselors do more effective evaluation work and thereby benefit both the profession and the students we serve.

References

American School Counselor Association. (2012). *The ASCA national model: A framework for school counseling programs* (3rd ed.). Alexandria, VA: Author.

American School Counselor Association. (2019). *The ASCA national model: A framework for school counseling programs* (4th ed.). Alexandria, VA: Author.

Authors

Dr. Michael S. Trevisan is dean of the College of Education and professor of educational psychology at Washington State University, Pullman, and the co-founder of the Learning and Performance Research Center. Dr. Trevisan co-authored the book *Evaluability Assessment: Improving Evaluation Quality and Use* (Sage). He has provided evaluation workshops to school districts, universities, and the United Nations Population Fund and at numerous professional meetings, both nationally and internationally. Dr. Trevisan is a founding member of the International Society for Policy Research and Evaluation in School-Based Counseling and a contributing author to the *International Handbook for Policy Research on School-based Counseling* (Springer, 2017). Dr. Trevisan has taught evaluation for pre-service school counseling students and worked with practicing school counselors to develop evaluation plans and carry out the work. In addition, he has written a number of articles that address the importance of evaluation for school counselors. His current work is focused on the development of evaluation capacity of school-based counselors and the development and implementation of school counseling policy research. This work has been carried out in such countries as India, Italy, South Korea, and the US.

Dr. John C. Carey is an emeritus professor of school counseling at the University of Massachusetts, Amherst, and the founder of the Ronald H. Fredrickson Center for School Counseling Outcome Research. Dr. Carey is an international leader in the evidence-based school counseling movement and has co-authored the influential book *Evidence-Based School Counseling: Making a Difference with Data-Driven Practices* (Corwin Press.) In addition, Dr. Carey has published numerous journal articles including statewide evaluations of the effectiveness of school counseling programs in Utah and Nebraska and a national study of the level of implementation of state school counseling models. Dr. Carey is currently the chair of the executive council of the International Society for Policy Research in School-based Counseling and served as the lead editor of the *International Handbook for Policy Research on School-based Counseling* (Springer). Dr. Carey has worked as a Fulbright specialist in India and Korea and has offered workshops in evaluation for counselors in Africa, Asia, Europe, Central America, and North America.

1 Toward a Conceptual Understanding of Evaluation for School Counselors

Questions to Consider

- What is the definition of evaluation?
- What are the purposes for evaluation?
- What is the connection between evaluation and the school counseling profession?
- What are the components to the school counseling evaluation framework?
- What are standards in program evaluation, and how can they be used?
- What is culturally responsive evaluation, and why is it important?

The Idea of Program Evaluation

This book is about the use of program evaluation by school counselors to help shape improvements of their program and services and demonstrate value to school personnel, families, and other stakeholders. When program evaluation is done well, improvement of the program and services is possible, informed by the information provided by the evaluation. Positive student outcomes as a result of the school counseling program are more likely. And school counselors can gain strong, sustained support for their program. In short, everyone benefits.

This book is unique because it makes connections between the discipline/ profession of evaluation and the discipline/profession of school counseling. In fact, we are advocating an interdisciplinary approach to program evaluation that enhances the profession of school counseling and increases the relevance for the field of evaluation, particularly for school counselors.

Evaluation as a discipline and profession is relatively young, with perhaps little more than 50 years in existence. As a consequence, many of the concepts, approaches, essential characteristics, and definitions are still emerging. As evaluators confront new challenges and develop new ways of addressing these challenges, new approaches replace old ones. This competition for ideas about evaluation and the rapid pace of development of the discipline make this an exciting time to do evaluation work.

Michael Scriven, one of the most prominent thinkers in evaluation, maintains that evaluation is a trans-discipline (Scriven, 2008). That is, while maintaining disciplinary features, evaluation is applied in a variety of other fields, such as school counseling. As different fields incorporate evaluation into the repertoire of professional practice, different ideas are developed about what constitutes evaluation and for what purposes it should be used. However, each profession defines evaluation somewhat differently, which can prevent broad understanding of the essential characteristics and purposes for evaluation.

The main goal of this book is to bring together the best thinking about evaluation and integrate these ideas with current practices of the school counseling field. We believe that evaluation has much to offer the professional school counselor. The concepts and ideas presented in this book are designed to provide the basis for school counselors to effectively evaluate their program and services.

As a starting point, the Joint Committee on Standards in Educational Evaluation (JCSEE) provides a comprehensive definition of program evaluation that has shown utility across a variety of fields, disciplines, and evaluators. Program evaluation is

- The systematic investigation of the quality of programs, projects, subprograms, subprojects, and/or any of their components or elements together or singly.
- For purposes of decision making, judgments, conclusions, findings, new knowledge, organizational development, and capacity building in response to the needs of identified stakeholders.
- Leading to improvement and/or accountability in the users' programs and systems.
- Ultimately contributing to organizational or social value (Yarbrough, Shulha, Hopson, & Caruthers, 2010; p. xxv).

This definition emphasizes that program evaluation is systematic. It is based on a clearly articulated evaluation plan that includes rigorous data collection protocols. In addition, program evaluation results must be used in some way. Evaluation information can be used to guide improvement of services, inform decisions about the merit or worth of a program, or provide accountability data to the general public. In the end, program evaluation should contribute something of value to society. It should lead to social betterment.

There is a lot packed into the aforementioned definition. Understanding what it all means for school counselors and learning how to accomplish its stated ends are the purposes of this book. One feature of the JCSEE Program Evaluation Standards important to note is that it was developed by a joint committee of representatives from a variety of disciplines and professions (Yarbrough et al., 2010). The American Counseling Association (ACA) has been a member of this joint committee for all three versions of the JCSEE Program Evaluation Standards. In short, a key counseling professional organization has recognized the importance of evaluation to the school counseling profession and provided input to develop evaluation standards that will meet the professional needs of school counselors. We will discuss the JCSEE Program Evaluation Standards in more detail later in this chapter.

Differences between Research and Evaluation

Further understanding of what evaluation is and is not, found in the literature, is to compare and contrast evaluation with social science research (e.g., Mathison, 2008; Walser & Trevisan, 2019). In many disciplines, evaluation is often confused with research. For school counseling students, this confusion is further compounded because evaluation is often taught in research methods courses. As a consequence, students can come away with the idea that evaluation is another form of research. Further, some authors argue that evaluation is applied research. That is, evaluation is simply the use of social science research methods in a particular context, (e.g., the evaluation of a school counseling program, intervention, or activity). After all, evaluation uses research methods to collect data that answer evaluation questions. So, it "looks and feels" like research.

However, the idea of program evaluation being simply another form of research falls short of an accurate and nuanced understanding of program evaluation, as it doesn't capture the many important features that are different from research. Most anyone deeply involved in evaluation today knows that stakeholders play an essential part and should have an integral role in developing some or all aspects of the evaluation. Research, applied or basic, is under no obligation to include stakeholders (Mathison, 2008). Thus, a key difference between research and evaluation is how each considers the involvement of stakeholders.

Another key difference is the purpose for which research and evaluation are conducted. As Alkin (2013) reflects, "For me, that distinction rests heavily on the difference between producing generalizable knowledge and providing information that will be helpful in improving specific programs" (p. 283). Mathison (2008) expands on the purpose of the research enterprise by arguing that research is focused on understanding the world. In contrast, evaluation is focused on determining the merit, worth, or significance of a program, project, or policy.

As you read this book and consider the ideas, pay particular attention to how evaluation differs from research. We think you will agree that there is uniqueness and depth to evaluation and that it is more than simply another form of research.

BOX 1.1

A key difference between research and evaluation is the need for stakeholder involvement in the evaluation process.

Purposes for Evaluation

Many prominent writers in evaluation have articulated a variety of purposes for evaluation (Owen & Rogers, 2007; Scriven, 1967; Stufflebeam & Coryn, 2014; Yarbrough et al., 2010). As different fields work to embrace and integrate evaluation within their professional practice, some purposes could offer more meaning than others. We believe that for school counselors, there are two purposes that likely have the most relevance. These are program improvement and impact assessment. Evaluation for program improvement is likely the most relevant purpose for school counseling professionals. Evaluation focused on whether or not the school counseling program and services are implemented as planned; the extent to which students, teachers, parents, and administrators are satisfied with services; and ways to improve the delivery of programs and services are the heart of program improvement. And, as Weiss (1988, 1998) has forcefully argued, evaluation data obtained by an evaluation plan developed by program staff (i.e., school counselors), about features of the program under their control, is one of the most powerful purposes within the evaluation enterprise.

The type of evaluation focused on program improvement is often referred to as formative evaluation, a term offered by Michael Scriven over 50 years ago (Scriven, 1967), a term that has endured the test of time as formative evaluation is used widely today. Evaluation methods used for formative evaluation include interviews, focus groups, checklists, observations, disaggregation of existing data, surveys, and questionnaires.

Assessment of impact is often the purpose for which many outside stakeholders are interested. Stakeholders such as school district administrators, statewide policymakers, and taxpayers often want to know whether or not expenditure of taxpayer dollars is having a payoff. They also want to know whether or not there is a positive difference in students that is attributable to receiving school counseling services. To this end, impact assessment focuses on documenting whether intended outcomes have been achieved and whether there are unintended positive or negative consequences of program implementation.

Assessment of impact is referred to as summative evaluation (Scriven, 1967). Summative evaluation is often associated with the idea of accountability. Summative evaluation is often done on a large-scale (e.g., collection of evaluation data from all school counseling programs in a school district or state, for example) and is often conducted by people external to the program. The assumption is that individuals external or unattached to the program likely have less vested in the program and therefore are thought of as being more objective. Often, sophisticated statistical techniques are used to compare students who received services or participated in an intervention to students who have not, all as a means to determine whether or not there are better outcomes for participating students.

An Evaluation Framework for School Counselors

We have conducted evaluation training for school counselors and counselor educators in the US (e.g., Trevisan & Carey, 2017) and internationally

(Carey & Trevisan, 2017; Lee & Trevisan, 2019; Trevisan & Carey, in press). Based on the school counseling and evaluation literature, the American School Counselor Association (ASCA, 2012) expectations, and our collective experience, we have developed a six-component evaluation framework that meets the formative and summative evaluation needs of school counselors as they work to improve their program and services and document outcomes. The evaluation framework includes the following components: (1) involve stakeholders, (2) theory of action, (3) evaluation questions, (4) evaluation design and method, (5) data analysis and findings, and (6) communicate and use evaluation results. Chapters 3–9 are devoted to each of the components. The component for data analysis and findings is divided into two chapters; these chapters (Chapters 7 and 8) are focused on quantitative and qualitative methods, respectively. Each of these chapters will provide the concepts so that you can effectively carry out each component of the school counseling evaluation framework. For now, each component will be briefly discussed here as a means to introduce the school counseling evaluation framework and provide an advanced organizer for subsequent chapters.

Component 1: Involve Stakeholders

Stakeholders are any individuals or groups that have a stake in the school counseling program and its evaluation. Involving stakeholders in one or more aspects of the evaluation is now thought central to conducting high-quality evaluation, evaluation that meets the standards of the field (Yarbrough et al., 2010). Stakeholders can help shape the evaluation to meet the needs and concerns of a wide variety of individuals and groups. The process of involving stakeholders in the evaluation will help establish the credibility of the findings and foster evaluation use.

As a school counselor, a key aspect of conducting evaluation of the school counseling program will be to identify stakeholders and engage them in the evaluation process. The ASCA National Model indicates the importance of stakeholder involvement through the school counseling advisory committee. We expand on the advisory committee requirement, advocate stakeholder involvement in more than an advisory role to the evaluation, and provide strategies to engage a wide variety of stakeholders in the evaluation process. The evaluation field has done significant work in this area and strategies for stakeholder involvement are readily accessible (e.g., Preskill & Jones, 2009; Walser & Trevisan, 2019).

Component 2: Theory of Action

The place to begin an evaluation of a school counseling program is with the development of a theory of action. A theory of action or program theory is not a social science theory that explains behavior and the like (Donaldson, & Lipsey, 2006). The theory of action is the logic of how a program is structured, resources are used, and activities are implemented, all in order to generate student behavioral and achievement outcomes. The theory of action is often depicted as a logic model in graphic form with inputs, activities, outputs, and outcomes.

The compelling feature of a logic model is that it requires the school counselor to work with stakeholders and make everyone's assumptions clear as to how people see the program working to support students (and teachers). Any differences would need to be negotiated so that resources and activities are implemented optimally to generate positive outcomes. There has been significant work done with logic models in school counseling (e.g., Martin & Carey, 2014). While the word "theory" can often convey to the practitioner something without relevance, in a now seminal paper written over 20 years ago, Weiss (1995), in characterizing the need for program theory, made the argument that "there is nothing more practical than a good theory" (p. 65). We think you'll agree.

Component 3: Evaluation Questions

Evaluation questions are questions about the things you and other stakeholders want to know about the program. Evaluation questions provide focus to the evaluation and signal the kind of data that should or could be collected. Both formative evaluation and summative evaluation have logical questions that could form the basis for developing more focused evaluation questions specific to your program. For formative evaluation, logical questions are

- Was the program implemented as planned?
- Was there a program component that was altered? What has occurred as a consequence?
- What is working well?
- What needs improvement?

Summative evaluation is focused on intended impact and unintended consequences. Logical questions include

- Were immediate outputs achieved?
- What is needed to report long-term outcomes?
- Were there unintended consequences due to the program? (positive or negative)
- What is the overall impact of the program?

As part of the initial phase of the evaluation, development of the evaluation questions is a place for stakeholders to insert what they see as essential to know about the program.

Component 4: Develop an Evaluation Design and Select Methods

The evaluation design and methods (data collection strategies) are chosen to answer the evaluation questions. Both quantitative and qualitative methods are often selected and used. These could include interviews, observations, questionnaires, and disaggregated student outcome data. To assess impact, research designs are often employed that compare before and after intervention data or compare students who have received services with those who have not. These comparisons would be made with experimental or quasi-experimental designs.

Both qualitative and quantitative methods can be tailored to address formative and summative evaluation questions. Our emphasis in this book is on formative evaluation as this is the kind of evaluation that will make most sense to school counselors and be of most use. However, we think some knowledge of summative evaluation could prove useful so that school counselors understand what summative evaluation could look like, what it entails, and how it could be used, particularly when external evaluation is conducted of the school counseling program. Moreover, the ASCA National Model requires summative evaluation by comparing student data in subsequent years to the baseline year, or before and after an intervention. Thus, knowledge and skill in summative evaluation will serve school counselors well as they deal with evaluation expectations within their professional practice.

Component 5: Data Analysis and Findings

Analyzing data collected through various evaluation designs and methods requires facility with a variety of methodological techniques. The techniques used depend on whether qualitative or quantitative data are being analyzed, as well as the evaluation design employed. Qualitative data collected through interviews, for example, require analysis of trends, themes, patterns, and outliers. Statistical methods are used to analyze quantitative data.

Evaluation findings can be thought of as answers to the evaluation questions. Findings provide the basis for program change recommendations.

Component 6: Communicate and Use the Evaluation Results

The ultimate aim of any program evaluation is to use the results toward improvement of school counseling policies, programs, and services that benefit students. Evaluation results can be communicated in a variety of ways and can be tailored to different audiences. This book will provide several useful ways to communicate evaluation results. In addition, the concept of evaluation use is the most researched topic in the evaluation literature (Christie, 2007). There are different ways to conceptualize evaluation use, and as a school counselor, it is important to understand how evaluations can be used so that you can navigate the often politically complex K-12 school organization and enterprise. Table 1.1 provides the components of the school counseling evaluation framework.

Standards for School Counseling Evaluation

While there are calls and recommendations for school counselors to conduct evaluations of their program and services, there has been little specifying what

Table 1.1 The six components of the school counseling evaluation framework

Number	Component
1	Involve stakeholders
2	Theory of action
3	Evaluation questions
4	Evaluation design and method
5	Data analysis and findings
6	Communicate and use the evaluation results

quality looks like in school counseling evaluation. As mentioned earlier, there exist standards that can be used to guide and assess the quality of evaluation of school counseling programs. And to reiterate, the ACA was a contributing member of the joint committee of professional organizations that developed the program evaluation standards. As the school counseling profession has maintained historical connections to the ACA, school counseling practitioners can be assured that their professional needs and concerns are represented.

The JCSEE Program Evaluation Standards are now in the third edition (Yarbrough et al., 2010). There are 30 standards organized in the following broad, quality categories, referred to as attributes:

- Utility
- Feasibility
- Propriety
- Accuracy
- Evaluation Accountability

The JCSEE Program Evaluation Standards can be thought of as rigorously developed concepts that signal quality in all aspects of an evaluation. The JCSEE Program Evaluation Standards reflect the collective professional judgment from a variety of disciplines about what constitutes high-quality professional evaluation work. The JCSEE Program Evaluation Standards can be flexibly applied within a given context (Yarbrough et al., 2010).

For school counselors, the evaluation framework we offer is specifically designed to address the JCSEE Program Evaluation Standards. In short, if the evaluation framework and processes are followed closely, school counselors will conduct quality evaluation of their program and services.

BOX 1.2

The JCSEE Program Evaluation Standards can be thought of as rigorously developed concepts that signal quality in all aspects of an evaluation.

Utility Standards

The utility standards refer to the usefulness of an evaluation. In Chapter 3, you will learn about the importance of identifying stakeholders and including stakeholders in the evaluation process so that the evaluation meets their information needs and concerns. Strategic stakeholder engagement will help to ensure that the evaluation meets utility standards as stakeholder engagement compels clarity of purpose, the inclusion of stakeholder information needs, and specification of the means to communicate the findings. For school counselors, stakeholders could include teachers, parents, students, building and school district administrators, and community members. In addition, Chapter 9 provides details and recommendations for communicating and using the evaluation. Communicating and using the evaluation is particularly relevant in meeting the utility standards. Table 1.2 lists the utility standards.

Feasibility Standards

Feasibility standards focus on the extent to which an evaluation addresses the effects of context, organizational constraints, and resources into the

Table 1.2 Utility standards

U1 Evaluator Credibility	Evaluations should be conducted by qualified people who establish and maintain credibility in the evaluation context.
U2 Attention to Stakeholders	Evaluations should devote attention to the full range of individuals and groups invested in the program and affected by its evaluation.
U3 Negotiated Purposes	Evaluation purposes should be identified and continually negotiated based on the needs of stakeholders.
U4 Explicit Values	Evaluations should clarify and specify the individual and cultural values underpinning purposes, processes, and judgments.
U5 Relevant Information	Evaluation information should serve the identified and emergent needs of stakeholders.
U6 Meaningful Processes and Products	Evaluations should construct activities, descriptions, and judgments in ways that encourage participants to rediscover, reinterpret, or revise their understandings and behaviors.
U7 Timely and Appropriate Communicating and Reporting	Evaluations should attend to the continuing information needs of their multiple audiences.
U8 Concern for Consequences and Influence	Evaluations should promote responsible and adaptive use while guarding against unintended negative consequences and misuse.

Source: From Yarbrough, D. B. et al. (2010). *The Program Evaluation Standards: A guide for evaluators and evaluation users* (3rd ed.). Thousand Oaks, CA: Corwin Press. Reproduced with permission from the Joint Committee for Standards in Educational Evaluation.

Table 1.3 Feasibility standards

F1 Project Management	Evaluations should use effective project management strategies.
F2 Practical Procedures	Evaluation procedures should be practical and responsive to the way the program operates.
F3 Contextual Viability	Evaluations should recognize, monitor, and balance the cultural and political interests and needs of individuals and groups.
F4 Resource Use	Evaluations should use resources effectively and efficiently.

Source: From Yarbrough, D. B. et al. (2010). *The Program Evaluation Standards: A guide for evaluators and evaluation users* (3rd ed.). Thousand Oaks, CA: Corwin Press. Reproduced with permission from the Joint Committee for Standards in Educational Evaluation.

school counseling evaluation. Another way to think about these standards is the determination of whether or not an evaluation of the school counseling program can be conducted in practical, cultural, and political terms. Stakeholder engagement will certainly help to address the cultural and political aspects of feasibility. School counselors will also need to think about their own time commitments and necessary resources and be thoughtful about weaving in the evaluation tasks and activities into their regular workload in order to meet feasibility standards. Table 1.3 lists the feasibility standards.

Propriety Standards

Propriety standards address the extent to which an evaluation maintains respect and dignity of all involved in the evaluation, particularly those from whom you are collecting data. Propriety includes clear communication and negotiated agreements so all involved know what commitments they are making toward the evaluation and the consequences for their involvement and are, thus, not surprised by the expectations.

Propriety also addresses human rights and elimination or minimization of risks to participants. In addition to clear communication and negotiated agreements, safeguards in the evaluation must also be implemented to protect human rights. Most school districts maintain some type of committee to review research being done with students and or school district staff. While we've argued that evaluation is not research, given that evaluation requires individuals provide feedback about either the program or themselves (like some research might ask), we think it is prudent to work with this committee to obtain school district permission to conduct the evaluation. Assuming the evaluation is done on a recurring basis, some type of blanket approval is recommended.

Research universities maintain an institutional review board (IRB) to review research that employs human subjects. The IRB is federally mandated for any institution that receives federal funding. Some school districts require human subjects review by an IRB (in lieu of a district committee that reviews research). The important point here is that within the IRB protocol, risks associated with collection of data from people must be identified and

Table 1.4 Propriety standards

P1 Responsive and Inclusive Orientation	Evaluations should be responsive to stakeholders and their communities.
P2 Formal Agreements	Evaluation agreements should be negotiated to make obligations explicit and take into account the needs, expectations, and cultural contexts of clients and other stakeholders.
P3 Human Rights and Respect	Evaluations should be designed and conducted to protect human and legal rights and maintain the dignity of participants and other stakeholders.
P4 Clarity and Fairness	Evaluations should be understandable and fair in addressing stakeholder needs and purposes.
P5 Transparency and Disclosure	Evaluations should provide complete descriptions of findings, limitations, and conclusions to all stakeholders, unless doing so would violate legal and propriety obligations.
P6 Conflicts of Interests	Evaluations should openly and honestly identify and address real or perceived conflicts of interests that may compromise the evaluation.
P7 Fiscal Responsibility	Evaluations should account for all expended resources and comply with sound fiscal procedures and processes.

Source: From Yarbrough, D. B. et al. (2010). *The Program Evaluation Standards: A guide for evaluators and evaluation users* (3rd ed.). Thousand Oaks, CA: Corwin Press. Reproduced with permission from the Joint Committee for Standards in Educational Evaluation.

processes articulated that minimize or eliminate these risks. Further, there are protected groups of people that require additional safeguards to avoid risks and maintain their dignity and rights as individuals associated with the school district. Native Americans, children, those who are incarcerated, and pregnant women are all protected groups. We could conceive of a school counseling program that has stakeholders from all of these groups of people. Thus, as you progress with your school counseling program evaluation, make sure that appropriate approvals for collecting data from people are obtained and that appropriate safeguards are in place to collect information from individuals who are members of these aforementioned groups. Table 1.4 lists the propriety standards.

Accuracy Standards

Accuracy standards refer to data reliability and validity, accuracy in communication, and justifiable conclusions. The elements involved in meeting accuracy standards include sound data collection protocols, responsive evaluation designs, and alignment of the evaluation and its conclusions with the purposes articulated.

Practicing school counselors may have had experience with program evaluations that were not accurate or did not align with the articulated purpose. In these situations, the evaluation may have caught some people off guard as

Table 1.5 Accuracy standards

A1 Justified Conclusions and Decisions	Evaluation conclusions and decisions should be explicitly justified in the cultures and contexts where they have consequences.
A2 Valid Information	Evaluation information should serve the intended purposes and support valid interpretations.
A3 Reliable Information	Evaluation procedures should yield sufficiently dependable and consistent information for the intended uses.
A4 Explicit Program and Context Descriptions	Evaluations should document programs and their contexts with appropriate detail and scope for the evaluation purposes.
A5 Information Management	Evaluations should employ systematic information collection, review, verification, and storage methods.
A6 Sound Design and Analyses	Evaluations should employ technically adequate designs and analyses that are appropriate for the evaluation purposes.
A7 Explicit Evaluation Reasoning	Evaluation reasoning leading from information and analyses to findings, interpretations, conclusions, and judgments should be clearly and completely documented.
A8 Communication and Reporting	Evaluation communications should have adequate scope and guard against misconceptions, biases, distortions, and errors.

Source: From Yarbrough, D. B. et al. (2010). *The Program Evaluation Standards: A guide for evaluators and evaluation users* (3rd ed.). Thousand Oaks, CA: Corwin Press. Reproduced with permission from the Joint Committee for Standards in Educational Evaluation.

they were not prepared for its ultimate use. Evaluation experiences like these generate mistrust of evaluation processes and can produce evaluation anxiety. In fact, evaluation anxiety is real and must be addressed if evaluation is going to be accepted and used (Donaldson, Gooer, & Scriven, 2002). One of the clearest ways to decrease evaluation anxiety, gain trust, and ultimately use the evaluation results to improve the program and services, is to maintain accuracy in all aspects of the evaluation. The standards provide guidance for an accurate evaluation. These issues will be discussed in further detail in subsequent chapters. Table 1.5 lists the accuracy standards.

Evaluation Accountability Standards

While it might seem redundant or awkward, even the evaluation itself should be accountable. The evaluation accountability standards communicate two ways to address accountability: (1) a complete evaluation report of the processes used, findings obtained, and recommendations made and (2) an internal or external review of the evaluation, referred to as meta-evaluation. The sixth component of the school counseling evaluation framework component, communicating and using the evaluation results, is one of the most relevant aspects of the evaluation framework for meeting the evaluation

Table 1.6 Evaluation accountability standards

E1 Evaluation Documentation	Evaluations should fully document their negotiated purposes and implemented designs, procedures, data, and outcomes.
E2 Internal Meta-evaluation	Evaluators should use these and other applicable standards to examine the accountability of the evaluation design, procedures employed, information collected, and outcomes.
E3 External Meta-evaluation	Program evaluation sponsors, clients, evaluators, and other stakeholders should encourage the conduct of external meta-evaluations using these and other applicable standards.

Source: From Yarbrough, D. B.et al. (2010). *The Program Evaluation Standards: A guide for evaluators and evaluation users* (3rd ed.). Thousand Oaks, CA: Corwin Press. Reproduced with permission from the Joint Committee for Standards in Educational Evaluation.

accountability standards. A comprehensive evaluation report will be one of the things addressed in implementing this component. Of course, most people are too busy and or uninterested in a full evaluation report. The benefit that a comprehensive report provides, however, is that it contains all aspects of the evaluation process. Should anyone have questions about the process or how the conclusions were drawn, for example, the report is a ready means to address these questions. Recommendations for making sure the evaluation itself is accountable will be provided in Chapter 9. Table 1.6 lists the evaluation accountability standards.

In developing an evaluation for your school counseling program, know that it is not necessary, prudent, or practical to meet every standard. A judgment on your part about which standards seem most relevant for your program evaluation will be required. And remember, by following the school counseling evaluation framework and recommendations offered in this book, meeting the most relevant standards to your evaluation is almost assured. A discussion about some of the most relevant standards within each of the evaluation framework chapters is provided.

Culturally Responsive Evaluation and the School Counseling Program

In the US, culture is a part of our educational programs and services. For example, in school districts across the US, several different languages are spoken among families and English is the second language or not spoken at all. The different languages indicate that there are different cultures present in the school community. Thus, culture is a dynamic that a school counselor must learn to navigate as they work to provide and evaluate the school counseling program and services.

Recognizing that any evaluation of educational programs in the US requires skills and abilities to navigate the cultural dynamics of the community, the American Evaluation Association developed competencies for evaluators. Referred to as the *Statement on Cultural Competence in Evaluation* (American

Evaluation Association, 2011), the document asserts the importance of recognizing the presence of culture in evaluation and, for those that evaluate programs, to find ways to develop and implement what is referred to as culturally responsive evaluation.

Interestingly for school counselors, the fields of counseling, psychology, and healthcare have done considerable work over the last 30+ years in recognizing the importance of culture to these professional practices. As a discipline and field, evaluation has learned from the work of the mental health fields to inform the *Statement on Cultural Competence in Evaluation* and to implore the evaluation community to work toward culturally responsive evaluation (Trevisan & Carey, 2019).

A strong recommendation in the literature on culturally responsive evaluation is to engage stakeholders in the evaluation. We will further discuss the importance of culture and ways to address culture in school counseling evaluation in Chapter 3, the chapter on the importance of stakeholder engagement. We will also provide recommendations on culturally responsive evaluation in the other chapters focused on the components of the school counseling evaluation framework.

Summary

This chapter developed the concept of evaluation by providing a rigorously constructed definition of evaluation, a definition that was constructed with broad input from many different professional organizations, including the ACA; distinguished evaluation from social science research; and detailed the purposes and types of evaluation relevant for school counselors. Further, an evaluation framework was provided that forms the basis for the evaluation work of school counselors and is the major focus of this book. The chapter made an initial connection between the disciplines and fields of school counseling and evaluation. Content highlights include

- Purposes for evaluation that include program improvement and assessment of impact.
- Formative evaluation and summative evaluation to address the above, respectively.
- Distinguishing features of evaluation that differentiate it from social science research which include stakeholder engagement and a focus on providing information for decision-making about a program or policy.
- An evaluation framework that includes (1) stakeholder involvement, (2) the development of a theory of action or logic model, (3) evaluation questions, (4) evaluation design and methods, (5) data analysis and findings, and (6) communication and use of the evaluation results.
- Standards that signal quality in evaluation work.
- The importance of conducting culturally responsive evaluation.

References

Alkin, M. C. (2013). Context-specific evaluation. In M. C. Alkin (Ed.), *Evaluation roots: A wider perspective of theorists' views and influences* (pp. 283–292). Los Angeles, CA: Sage Publications.

American Evaluation Association. (2011). *Public statement on cultural competence in evaluation*. Fairhaven, MA: Retrieved from www.eval.org

American School Counselor Association. (2012). *The ASCA national model: A framework for school counseling programs* (3rd ed.). Alexandria, VA: Author.

Carey, J. & Trevisan, M.S. (2017, October). Evaluation in support of school counseling in Italian schools. *Workshop Presented at Pratiche Educative, Di Cura E Benessere (Counseling in Action), Annual Meeting of Continuando a Crescere*, Verona, Italy.

Christie, C. A. (2007). Reported influence of evaluation data on decision makers' actions: An empirical examination. *American Journal of Evaluation, 28*(1), 8–25.

Donaldson, S. I., Gooler, L. E., & Scriven, M. (2002). Strategies for managing evaluation anxiety: Toward a psychology of program evaluation. *American Journal of Evaluation, 23*(3), 261–273.

Donaldson, S. I. & Lipsey, M. W. (2006). Roles for theory in contemporary evaluation practice: Developing practical knowledge. In I. F. Shaw, J. C. Green, & M. M. Mark (Eds.), *The Sage handbook of evaluation* (pp. 56–75). Thousand Oaks, CA: Sage.

Lee, S. M. & Trevisan, M. S. (2019). Evaluation in support of school counseling in Korea: A proposal. *Korean Journal of Education policy, 16*(1), 63–80.

Martin, I. & Carey, J. (2014). Development of a logic model to guide evaluations of the ASCA National Model for school counseling programs. *The Professional Counselor, 4*(5), 455–466.

Mathison, S. (2008). What is the difference between evaluation and research - and why do we care? In N. L. Smith & P. R. Brandon (Eds.), *Fundamental issues in evaluation* (pp. 183–196). New York, NY: Guilford Press.

Owen, J. M. & Rogers, P. J. (2007). *Program evaluation: Forms and approaches*. London, UK: Sage.

Preskill, H. & Jones, N. (2009). *A practical guide for engaging stakeholders in developing evaluation questions. Robert Wood Johnson Foundation Evaluation Series*. Retrieved from www.rwjf.org

Scriven, M. (1967). The methodology of evaluation. In R. E. Stake (Ed.), *Perspectives on curriculum evaluation (American Educational Research Association monograph series on evaluation, No. 1)*. Chicago: Rand McNally.

Scriven, M. (2008). The concept of a transdiscipline: And evaluation as a transdiscipline. *Journal of Multidisciplinary Evaluation, 5*(10), 65–66.

Stufflebeam, D. L. & Coryn, C. L. S. (2014). *Evaluation theory, models, and applications* (2nd ed.). San Francisco, CA: Jossey-Bass.

Trevisan, M.S. & Carey, J. (2017, March). Program Evaluation for School Counselors. *Workshop presentation at the Fifth Annual Evidence-Based School Counselors National Conference*, San Diego, CA.

Trevisan, M.S. & Carey, J.C. (2019). Evaluating intercultural programs and interventions. In A. Portera, R. Moodley, & M. Milani (Eds.), *Intercultural mediation, counselling and psychotherapy in Europe*. Cambridge Scholars, UK. Edited book under review.

Trevisan, M. S. & Carey, J. C. (in press). Evaluation in support of counseling in Italian schools. Revista Italiana di Counseling.

Walser, T. M. & Trevisan, M. S. (2019). *Completing your evaluation dissertation, thesis, or final project.* Los Angeles, CA: Sage. Manuscript under review.

Weiss, C. H. (1988). Evaluation for decisions: Is anybody there? Does anybody care? *Evaluation Practice,* 9(1), 5–19.

Weiss, C. H. (1995). Nothing as practical as good theory: Exploring theory-based evaluation for comprehensive community initiatives for children and families. In J. P. Connell, A. C. Kubisch, L. B. Schorr, & C. H. Weiss (Eds.), *New approaches to evaluating community initiatives: Concepts, methods, and contexts* (pp. 65–92) Washington, DC: Aspen Institute.

Weiss, C. H. (1998). Have we learned anything new about the use of evaluation? *American Journal of Evaluation,* 19(1), 21–33.

Yarbrough, D. B., Shulha, L. M., Hopson, R. K., & Caruthers, F. A. (2010). *The program evaluation standards: A guide for evaluators and evaluation users* (3rd ed.). Thousand Oaks, CA: Corwin Press.

2 Evaluation and the School Counseling Program and Profession

Questions to Consider

- What is the difference between whole program and activity level program evaluation?
- What are the similarities and differences between program evaluation and data-based decision-making?
- What are the major program evaluation-related activities under the ASCA National Model?
- What are the major strengths and limitations of program evaluation under the ASCA National Model?
- What are the major evaluation practices that should be added to ASCA National Model programs to strengthen program evaluation?
- What are the professional standards and expectations for school counselors as evaluators?

Vignette

This vignette and subsequent vignettes illustrate the implementation of the key program evaluation features of the ASCA National Model (noted in *italics*) and features (noted in **bold**) that can be added to improve the quality of information and the utility of the program evaluation by connecting school counseling program evaluation with effective practices from the field of evaluation.

The school counselors at Rocky Mountain High School have developed and implemented an ASCA National Model program. They initially conducted a *school counseling program assessment* and a *use-of-time assessment* to make sure that all the essential components of the ASCA National Model program are in place and that they are allocating time resources properly. **In addition, they used surveys and focus groups to gather data on stakeholder satisfaction from students, parents, teachers, and administrators**. **Using the combined data**, they established *short- and long-term goals* for improving the program. **They conducted a needs assessment and** completed a *school data profile analysis* to identify needed foci for activities and interventions. They selected several of the most critically important foci, developed interventions based on **the logic model they developed** and **formatively evaluated each**, making corrections and modifications where necessary to ensure that they were maximally effective. The next year they developed *action plans* for these interventions, collected pre-post data, and **analyzed these data statistically** to determine the success of these interventions. They developed *action plan reports* and shared these results with their *advisory council*, school administration, and the school community. They have also collected follow-up **stakeholder satisfaction data** and completed yearly *program goal analyses* to monitor program goal attainment and make corrections for the next year. They are considering applying for *recognized ASCA National Model program status.*

Program Evaluation and the School Counseling Program

As Chapter 1 illustrates, program evaluation uses systematic methods to produce information that is used to improve services and demonstrate the value of these services to stakeholders. When speaking of program evaluation in the context of school counseling, some semantic confusion results from the language differences that exist between the two fields. School counseling is now considered to be a comprehensive, organized **program** within schools that includes a variety of interventions, services, and activities that are intended to promote the cognitive, personal/social, and career development of students. Evaluators consider **program evaluation** to be concerned with the evaluation of both the overall program and its constituent parts. For school counseling, this means evaluating both the overall program and the individual interventions, services, and activities that it includes. Naturally, an evaluation of a whole counseling program requires a more complex approach than the evaluation of its specific deliverables.

The ASCA National Model (ASCA, 2012) includes both whole program level and specific activity level program evaluation components. For example, at the whole program level, the ASCA National Model recommends a *School Counseling Program Assessment* that audits the program to determine whether or not the essential elements of the ASCA National Model are being implemented. The *School Counseling Program Assessment* reflects an aspect of formative evaluation, a test of whether or not all the putative active ingredients associated with the program are in place.

At the service level, the ASCA National Model recommends *Action Reports* that include information on changes in student behavior and performance that are expected to be associated with specific interventions or activities. These *Action Reports* are intended to be summative evaluations, designed to produce impact data on the outcomes and benefits of specific activities or interventions (curriculum-based, small-group, and closing-the-gap) to stakeholders in a form that will persuasively demonstrate their value.

This book uses program evaluation to refer to whole program level and activity level evaluation in school counseling, explicates the important conceptual and methodological differences that exist between the two levels, and highlights the differences between formative evaluation and summative evaluation approaches at each level.

School Counseling Program Evaluation and Data-Based Decision-Making

Some confusion also exists between **program evaluation** and **data-based decision-making** in the context of the school counseling program. In recent years, both public school administration and the field of school counseling have been strongly influenced by management and evaluation practices that were developed to facilitate school reform within the K-12 education sector. Data-based decision-making (DBDM) is such a practice. DBDM can be defined as "the process of collecting, analyzing, reporting and using data for school improvement" (Dahlkemper, 2002, p. 1). DBDM methods became popular as a consequence of state and national efforts to improve public education through standards-based reform. These methods emphasized the use of existing school data to identify targets toward which school improvement-related activities were to be directed and the subsequent monitoring of these data elements to determine whether or not the activities were having their desired impact (Dimmitt, Carey, & Hatch, 2007).

When thinking about DBDM, there are three characteristics to keep in mind. First, DBDM typically focuses much more on documenting impact (summative evaluation) than on improving the processes that produce outcomes, and it is best applied in situations where there is a strong association between a given program activity and some existing piece of school data. DBDM is much less useful in formative evaluation situations where the immediate goal of the evaluation is to improve the intervention or activity and in situations where there may not be an immediate and obvious change in an existing school data element that can be expected to be associated with a specific activity or intervention. Second, DBDM also typically eschews more complex statistical analysis methods in favor of simple pre-post comparisons using percentages. Consequently, it is best suited to situations where there is little variability ("noise") in the data and where large pre-post changes in the data can be expected. Third, DBDM relies heavily on the use of existing school data. It is ill-suited for evaluation situations where new data needs to be collected in order to conduct a fair test of an intervention or activity or the program as a whole.

The development of the ASCA National Model (ASCA, 2003; 2012) was heavily influenced by the K-12 sector's investments of DBDM prompted by the standards-based educational reform movement. As we will see, the program evaluation practices of the ASCA National Model have strengths and shortcomings that result from this attachment to DBDM.

Historical Roots of School Counseling Models of Practice

Evolution of Counseling in Schools

School counselors have existed in US schools for well over 100 years. However, the goals of school counseling, the nature of the work of school counselors, and how this work is planned, organized, and evaluated has changed over the years, in part to meet school and national needs at different times. The original (1900s) impetus for having counselors in schools was to provide support for students in making vocational choices and finding suitable employment.

Expansion of the work of school counselors was initiated in the 1920s in response to the mental hygiene, psychometric, and child study movements and became more concerned with the mental health and psychological adjustment of students. The Vocational Education Act of 1946 provided support that led to a dramatic expansion of vocationally focused counseling in schools. The National Defense Education Act (NDEA) of 1958 was enacted in response to the perception that the US lagged behind the Soviet Union in the development of cold war technology. This resulted in tremendous growth of school counseling by providing a massive infusion of support for school counseling units in state departments of education, counselor education programs in universities, and school counselors in public schools (Gysbers, 2010).

The rationale behind NDEA's support was that school counselors were needed in US schools to prospect for engineering and science talent and encourage able students to pursue careers that would contribute to the national defense. With the waxing of nondirective counseling approaches in the 1960s, school counseling became more oriented toward the promotion of the human potential and mental health of students and more committed to relationship-oriented counseling interventions.

Rather than choosing between vocational and mental health orientations, the school counseling profession opted to adopt a comprehensive model that embraced both foci within the school counselor role. In addition, the profession embraced both a primary prevention orientation and a remedial counseling orientation. By the 1980s, school counselors had a very complex role that encompassed a wide range of activities, including one-on-one mental health counseling, career and vocational counseling, supportive group counseling, psych-educational prevention programming, career education, academic planning, work transition counseling, college transition counseling, parent education, and parent and teacher consultation.

To make matters even more complex, school administrators often had views about how school counselors should spend their time which differed from the orthodox view of the profession. As compared to teachers, the value that school counselors, acting with their self-chosen broad role, add to the education of students is less readily apparent. It was (and still is) tempting for administrators to assign school counselors responsibilities that needed to be accomplished to operate the school effectively (e.g., monitoring students' lunchroom behavior) that were not related to the self-defined role of school counselors and detracted from their ability to perform that role. Since at least the 1980s, school counselors have felt the need to justify the value of their professional work in schools. This was the impetus for the promotion of program evaluation of school counseling programs and services.

Comprehensive Developmental School Counseling

School counseling grew in breadth and complexity. In the 1980s, the reformulation of school counseling as a program rather than as a position in a school gained primacy.

Three different models for school counseling programs emerged: Comprehensive Developmental Guidance (CDG) (Gysbers & Henderson, 1988), Developmental Guidance and Counseling (Myrick, 1987), and Results-Based Guidance (Johnson & Johnson, 1991). To a great extent the need for program evaluation in school counseling began in this period with a shift in thinking about school counseling as an organized program within a school rather than as a position that people occupy.

All three historical models maintain counseling as a program within schools that delivered a complex array of preventive and remedial services with the intention to promote student development across a wide range of domains, often expressed as academic, career, and personal/social development. All three models included program evaluation activities that were to be conducted by school counselors themselves or in collaboration with an external evaluator. These program evaluation tasks and activities reflected commonly accepted evaluation practices of the time. Gysbers and Henderson (1988), for example, included relatively sophisticated suggestions on how to (1) formatively evaluate the program through the use of implementation standards, (2) identify unintended negative and positive "side effects" of program implementation, (3) measure student learning and behavior change, (4) decide on an appropriate evaluation design (e.g., "observational," single group, control group), (5) select and develop evaluation instruments, and (6) share evaluation results with stakeholders. It is clear that these early models expected that school counselors would develop expertise in program evaluation and be able to exercise judgment and critical thinking as they designed, conducted, and reported the results of their program evaluations.

ASCA National Model

The ASCA National Model for school counseling programs is the most influential approach to the design, organization, management, and evaluation of a comprehensive developmental school counseling program. Martin, Carey, and DeCoster (2009) reported that by 2009, 33 states had either adopted state models with ASCA National Model features or modernized their state model to reflect the ASCA National Model content. The ASCA National Model (ASCA, 2006) was originally developed in the late 1990s as a political response to perceived threats to the school counseling profession resultant from adoption of widespread standards-based models of education across the US. Many school counselors felt threatened by standards-based education reform because it focused almost exclusively on the goal of promoting academic achievement (as opposed to more traditional counseling goals such as vocational choice, college placement, social skills development, self-knowledge development, and mental health). The ASCA National Model was developed through a blending of CDG (Gysbers & Henderson, 1988), Developmental Guidance and Counseling (Myrick, 1987), and Results-Based Guidance (Johnson & Johnson, 1991). It was intended to create a common program model that would include the essential elements of the three existing models and to align the school counseling program with the principles and practices of standards-based education. In addition, ASCA sought to create a unified model to eliminate competition among proponents of the three traditional models. Both the alignment with standards-based education and the creation of a unified model for the school counseling program were seen as necessary responses to a climate that was perceived as threatening to school counselors and the profession.

The ASCA National Model was also influenced by the accountability and evidence-based practice movements advocates who promoted measuring the results of school counseling activities and using these results to both improve the program and demonstrate its value to stakeholders. However, the approach to program evaluation advocated by the ASCA National Model is relatively simplistic compared with the approach advocated for by leaders of the comprehensive school counseling, accountability, or evidence-based practice movements (Dimmitt, Carey, & Hatch, 2007; Gysbers & Henderson, 1988; Sink, 2009).

The current third-edition ASCA National Model (ASCA, 2012) retains all of the essential features of the original model including a "cookbook" approach to model implementation and evaluation. This approach was necessary because school counselors do not typically receive adequate training in either program management or program evaluation. The ASCA National Model simplified both of these activities through the creation of templates and forms that school counselors can follow to support program management and evaluation. The ASCA National Model rooted its program evaluation approach in data-based decision-making, which had emerged as a credible practice in standards-based school planning and management in US public schools.

The ASCA National Model includes program evaluation activities in both the management and accountability components. These activities are targeted at both the whole program level and the service level. Table 2.1 describes the major ASCA National Model tools related to evaluation and their purposes.

Consistent with many data-based decision-making approaches, the ASCA National Model relies heavily on the use of existing institutional data for program management and evaluation. In order to collect short-term program results data, school counselors need to be able to construct simple pre-post questionnaires related to the specific instructional objectives of the activity. However, existing institutional data are used as measures of impact. A group counseling intervention might, for example, be evaluated in terms of pre-post

Table 2.1 ASCA National model tools related to evaluation

Tool	Purpose
School Counseling Program Assessment	Determine the extent to which the prescribed elements of the ASCA National Model are present in the school counseling program.
Use-of-Time Assessment	Document of the amount of counselor time spent on each of the ASCA National Model's four categories of service delivery.
Yearly *Program Goals Analysis*	Determine whether or not the goals for program are being met and whether or not program improvements are being made.
School Data Profile	Compile data that includes all the important student achievement measures obtainable from school data (e.g., attendance rates) so that these data can be used to identify problems that require the attention of school counselors.
Developing *Action Plans*	Describe the implementation and evaluation processes for specific interventions, activities, or services (e.g., curriculum-based guidance, small-group counseling interventions, and closing-the-gap interventions) that are intended to address identified problems.
Action Plan Reports	Sharing the results of the above mentioned evaluation-related activities with stakeholders including parents and teachers.

changes in participating students' abilities to identify key concepts taught in the group, and pre-post changes in participating students' numbers of days absent. In both cases, inspection of percentage change (e.g., percentage of students able to identify key concepts before AND after instruction) and graphic representations of change would be considered as adequate evidence for effectiveness.

BOX 2.1

The ASCA National Model includes many tools related to program evaluation.

Underemphasized Aspects of Program Evaluation

While the ASCA National Model program evaluation practices reflect a significant advancement for the field of school counseling, there are several areas where they fall short of the most effective evaluation practices. These include

- An underutilization of input from the beneficiaries and other stakeholders of counseling services (students, parents, teachers, and administrators) in guiding program design and content, modifying program directions, and evaluating improvement.

- An underutilization of the formative evaluation of interventions, activities, and services.
- A lack of utilization of logic models in planning and evaluation.
- An overreliance on existing school data in planning and evaluation.
- An overemphasis of very simple forms of quantitative data analysis.
- An absence of the use of potentially powerful qualitative evaluation approaches.
- An overreliance on the advisory council for obtaining information on stakeholder preference and for disseminating evaluation results.

It is not clear that the ASCA National Model's simplified approach to program evaluation is adequate for the task of producing the highest quality and most useful information. Stakeholder needs, perspectives on the program, and satisfaction with services are not adequately assessed. The lack of use of more sophisticated evaluation designs (both qualitative and quantitative) limits the quality, utility, and value of the obtained information in many evaluations. The lack of sophistication in statistical analysis is likely to contribute to bad decisions through the inappropriate acceptance of false-positive findings and the inappropriate rejection of false-negative findings. The de-emphasis of formative evaluation is likely to result in inadequate implementation of activities and interventions. The overreliance on institutional data (and the related lack of sophistication in selecting and creating psychometrically sound evaluation measures) will result in limitations in what can be evaluated. Overreliance on institutional data will also create problems with using outcome measures that are misaligned with program components and activities. In short, the program evaluation component of the ASCA National Model would be found to be lacking when compared to the JCSEE Program Evaluation Standards (Yarbrough et al., 2010). Limitations in the ASCA National Model's approach to program evaluation seem to have resulted from the perceived need to produce a very simplified approach to evaluation and from a lack of grounding of this approach in widely accepted standards and approaches to program evaluation. Connecting school counseling program evaluation to best practices in the field of evaluation is needed to improve the quality of the information use for program improvement and professional advocacy.

Program Evaluation and School Counseling Professional Standards

ASCA

The school counseling profession supports the importance of school counselors having some competence in program evaluation. The current ASCA Ethical Standards for School Counselors (ASCA, 2016) indicate that in order to provide students with the services available through a comprehensive development program, school counselors are ethically obliged to

- Use school and student data to identify needs and needed interventions.
- Collect and analyze school data to determine the progress and effectiveness of the school counseling program.
- Share evaluation information on program effectiveness with stakeholders.

ASCA School Counselor Competencies (ASCA, n.d.), a statement on the competencies needed in order to implement the ASCA National Model school counseling program, also indicates that school counselors need to be able to engage in program evaluation activities. For example, the statement indicates that counselors need to be able to

- Use data to evaluate program effectiveness and to determine program needs.
- Analyze school data and results reports to determine program needs and effectiveness.
- Use formal and informal program evaluation methods to improve the school counseling program.
- Evaluate curriculum-based, small-group, and closing-the-gap activities.
- Use evaluation results obtained for program improvement.
- Use evaluation results to demonstrate the contributions of the school counseling program to student achievement.
- Share the program evaluation results with administrators, stakeholders, and the school community.

In addition, national school counselor accrediting bodies and state licensing boards support the necessity of school counselors being prepared to engage in program evaluation.

BOX 2.2

Professional standards recognize that school counselors must be proficient in program evaluation.

CACREP

The Council for the Accreditation of Counseling and Related Educational Programs (CACREP) is a national organization that accredits university-based school counseling programs. CACREP accredits school counselor training programs along with other counseling specializations. There are currently 259 CACREP accredited master's level school counselor training programs (CACREP, n.d.).

In order to achieve CACREP accreditation, training programs must demonstrate alignment with CACREP's standards. These standards include content related to program evaluation; however, critical content that is unique to program evaluation is missing from the standards, largely because the standards conflate research with program evaluation and were heavily weighted toward requiring research competencies (Trevisan, 2000; Trevisan, Carey, Martin, & Sundarajan, in press). The current research and evaluation standards (CACREP, 2016) indicate that training programs must provide curricular experiences that teach

- The importance of research in advancing the counseling profession, including how to critique research to inform counseling practice.
- Identification of evidence-based counseling practices.
- Needs assessment.
- Development of outcome measures for counseling programs.
- Evaluation of counseling interventions and programs.
- Qualitative, quantitative, and mixed research methods.
- Designs used in research and program evaluation.
- Statistical methods used in conducting research and program evaluation.
- Analysis and use of data in counseling.
- Ethical and culturally relevant strategies for conducting, interpreting, and reporting the results of research and program evaluation.

Although less specific than the ASCA competencies, the CACREP standards clearly indicate the intention that school counselors (and in fact all counselors) are competent in program evaluation.

State Licensing and Certification

In addition to influencing counselor training through its accreditation process, CACREP has influenced state licensing and certification standards for school counselors. Many states have incorporated the CACREP standards (including the research and evaluation standards) in their curricular requirements for initial school counselor licensure or certification (Trevisan et al., in press). All 50 states and the District of Columbia issue licenses or certificates to counselors that enable them to be employed in public schools. Trevisan et al. (in press) found that 43 states (including the District of Columbia) require some evidence of program evaluation competence for the initial school counselor licensure applicants in the form of mandated CACREP standards for their graduate program, specified required course content in program evaluation, and/or passing a licensure test that contains some items that assess program evaluation. Unfortunately, Trevisan et al. (in press) also found that most states' curricular requirements in program evaluation were relatively weak. Furthermore, in a follow-up study of the licensure examinations used by 31 states, Carey, Martin, Harrington, and Trevisan (2018) found that program evaluation content was insufficient to ensure that applicants who passed the examination actually had the requisite knowledge and skills to conduct program evaluations.

School Counseling Program Evaluation Beyond the National Model

Up to this point, our discussion of school counseling and program evaluation has focused a good deal on the ASCA National Model (ASCA, 2012) because of the prominence of this model within the profession. While the ASCA National Model is currently the dominant model in the US (Martin, Carey, & DeCoster, 2009), it is not the only model for the organization and management of school counseling programs. In a recent analysis of US school counseling policy research, Carey and Martin (2017, p. 411) questioned whether the ASCA National Model is appropriate across the wide range of school contexts in the US and suggested that "A revisioning of school counseling in the US is necessary in order to establish an approach to practice that fits with current education policy objectives and models of schooling; and that frees practice from the historical constraints that limit possibilities for development and change." Several alternative models of school counseling have been recently developed (Astramovich, Hoskins, & Bartlett, 2010; McMahon, Mason, Daluga-Guenther, & Ruiz, 2014; McMahon, Lee, & Goodnough, 2011). While it is prudent at this point to learn the specific program evaluation practices advocated by the ASCA National Model, it is also wise to develop a deeper level competence in program evaluation. Though program models will continue to evolve and change, often in unpredictable ways, one thing is certain, school counselors will always need to engage in program evaluation to improve their services and prove their value.

Summary

School counseling is best considered to be a distinct program within schools that delivers a broad range of services to support the academic, personal/social, and career development of students. School counselors need to be able to evaluate the program as a whole and its constituent interventions, services, and activities. Information from program evaluation is needed to improve the program and to demonstrate its value to stakeholders.

The ASCA National Model (2012), which is the most influential current program model, was heavily influenced by data-based decision-making approaches to school management and includes many program evaluation-related components. ASCA National Model program evaluation practices have limitations that can be overcome through the addition of best practices from the field of evaluation.

The school counseling profession suggests that all school counselors need to be engaged in program evaluation and have the necessary competencies to do so. CACREP program accreditation standards and state licensure requirements endorse the importance of school counselors being competent in program evaluation. However, both need some development and revision in order to maximize their abilities to promote skill development and quality assurance.

At this point in the development of the profession, it is wise for school counselors to learn the specific program evaluation practices advocated by the ASCA National Model, and to also develop a deeper level competence in program evaluation that will serve them well in the future.

References

American School Counselor Association. (n.d.). ASCA School Counselor Competencies. Retrieved from: https://www.schoolcounselor.org/asca/media/asca/home/SCCompetencies.pdf

American School Counselor Association. (2003). *The ASCA national model: A framework for school counseling programs.* Alexandria, VA: Author.

American School Counselor Association. (2006). *The ASCA national model: A framework for school counseling programs* (2nd ed.). Alexandria, VA: Author.

American School Counselor Association. (2012). *The ASCA national model: A framework for school counseling programs* (3rd ed.). Alexandria, VA: Author.

American School Counselor Association. (2016). *ASCA ethical standards for school counselors.* Alexandria, VA: Author.

Astramovich, R. L., Hoskins, W. J., & Bartlett, K. A. (2010). *Rethinking the organization and delivery of counseling in schools.* Vistas Online, Article 78. American Counseling Association.

Carey, J. C. & Martin, I. (2017). Policy research on school-based counseling in the United States: Establishing a policy research agenda. In Carey, J. C., Harris, B., Lee, S. M., & Aluede, O. (Eds.), *International handbook for policy research in school-based counseling.* New York: Springer.

Carey, J. C., Martin, I., Harrington, K., & Trevisan, M. S. (2018). Competence in program evaluation and research assessed by state school counselor licensure examinations. *Professional School Counseling, 22*(1), 1–11.

Council for Accreditation of Counseling and Related Educational Programs CACREP (n.d.). CACREP director of accredited programs. Retrieved from http://www.cacrep.org/directory/

Council for Accreditation of Counseling and Related Educational Programs (2016). CACREP Standards. Retrieved from http://www.cacrep.org/wp-content/uploads/2016/06/2016-Standards-with-Glossary-rev-2.2016.pdf

Dahlkemper, L. (2002). School board leadership: Using data for school improvement. *National School Board Association Research Policy Brief, 2*(1), 1–4.

Dimmitt, C., Carey, J., & Hatch, T. (2007). *Evidence- based school counseling: Making a difference with data-driven practices.* Thousand Oaks, CA: Corwin Press.

Gysbers, N. (2010). *Remembering the past, shaping the future: A history of school counseling.* Alexandria, VA: American School Counseling Association.

Gysbers, N. & Henderson, P. (1988). *Developing and managing your school guidance program.* Alexandria, VA: American Association for Counseling and Development.

Johnson, S. K. & Johnson, C. D. (1991). The new guidance: A systems approach to pupil personnel programs. *California Association of Counseling and Development, 11,* 5–14.

Martin, I., Carey, J. C., & DeCoster, K. (2009). A national study of the current status of state school counseling models. *Professional School Counseling, 12,* 378–386.

McMahon, H. G., Lee, V. V., & Goodnough, G. E. (2011). Systemic data-driven school counseling practice and programming for equity. In B. T. Erford (Ed.), *Transforming the school counseling profession* (3rd ed.). Boston, MA: Pearson Merrill Prentice-Hall.

McMahon, H. G., Mason, E. C. M., Daluga-Guenther, N., & Ruiz, A. (2014). An ecological model of professional school counseling. *Journal of Counseling and Development*, 92(4), 459–471.

Myrick, R. D. (1987) *Developmental guidance and counseling: A practical approach.* Minneapolis, IN: Educational Medial Corporation.

Sink, C. A. (2009). School counselors as accountability leaders: Another call for action. *Professional School Counseling*, 13, 68–74.

Trevisan, M. S. (2000). The status of program evaluation expectations in state school counselor certification requirements. *American Journal of Evaluation*, 21(1), 81–94.

Trevisan, M. S., Carey, J. C., Martin, I., & Sundarajan, N. (in press). School Counselor State Licensure Requirements and Professional Accreditation. *Journal of School-Based Counseling Policy and Evaluation*.

Yarbrough, D. B., Shulha, L. M., Hopson, R. K., & Caruthers, F. A. (2010). *The program evaluation standards: A guide for evaluators and evaluation users* (3rd ed.). Thousand Oaks, CA: Corwin Press.

3 Involving Stakeholders

Questions to Consider

- What is a stakeholder and why are they important to evaluation?
- What are the stakeholder groups for your school counseling program?
- Why would they be interested in the evaluation of your program?
- How would you work to maintain stakeholders' commitment to the evaluation?
- How would you organize a large number of stakeholders to engage in an evaluation of your school counseling program?
- Given competing interests among stakeholder groups, how can you work to maintain fairness in the evaluation of your school counseling program?

Vignette

The school counseling program at Maple Valley High School has *implemented the ASCA National Model for the last five years.* The high school has a *fully functioning and active advisory council.* Given the large size of the high school and the fact that there are 80 different languages spoken in homes of the students, the advisory council has taken on an important role in giving voice to the many stakeholder groups in the high school community for school counseling services.

School counselors at the high school have followed the *ASCA National Model* (ASCA, 2012) *guidelines for advisory councils.* There is a *chairperson and term limits for this 20-member group. Meeting agendas and minutes are developed and written for each meeting.* The school counselors carefully consider potential advisory council members for their commitment to school counseling services and their skills and abilities in working productively with a diverse group of people. **For the school counseling program evaluation, ancillary groups of stakeholders are established in order to ensure representation from school and community stakeholders.**

In addition to providing feedback on program goals and objectives and examining disaggregated school data, as recommended by ASCA, **the school counselors have included the advisory council and ancillary groups in the development, implementation, and analysis of the school counseling**

program evaluation. To do this, an outside evaluation consultant is hired to provide training to council members and stakeholders and help the school counselors organize the evaluation tasks and activities. While there is extra work involved, **school counselors feel that the benefits to the school counseling program and services are worth the extra work in having stakeholders closely involved with the evaluation.**

Stakeholders and Evaluation

Stakeholders are individuals and groups with a vested interest in the program and its services. By implication, stakeholders are vested in the evaluation of the program as well. A hallmark of the development of the field of evaluation is the role and place of stakeholders. Stakeholder involvement in the evaluation is now commonplace and recommended as sound professional evaluation practice (Preskill & Jones, 2009; Yarbrough et al., 2010). The benefits to school counseling program evaluation deserve attention. When done well, evaluations support and foster good decisions about the school counseling program and services. Stakeholder involvement helps to ensure that evaluations reflect stakeholder needs and concerns about the program and, in turn, increase the likelihood that the evaluation findings will be acted on. Also, addressing the needs and concerns of stakeholders will ensure that the school counseling program and services will be accountable to the people it serves and the community in which it resides. It will therefore be important to you as a school counselor to identify all stakeholders and what their needs and concerns are for the program and its evaluation.

School Counseling Stakeholders

There is surprisingly little written about program stakeholders in the school counseling literature. What is written has largely to do with advisory councils as envisioned by the ASCA National Model (ASCA, 2012). The ASCA National Model recommends that

> The broader the representation on the advisory council, the more the group's work will accurately reflect the community's values, concerns and interests. Ideally, members of the advisory council reflect the diversity of the community and include students, parents, teachers, school counselors, administrators, school board members, and business and community members. (ASCA, 2012; p. 47)

We think more attention to stakeholders is needed as stakeholders in school counseling could be strong advocates for the school counseling program and services. Tapping into this potential through effective interactions with stakeholders could have a real payoff for your school counseling program. And as previously mentioned, we think that the school counseling program should be accountable to the people it serves and the groups that have a stake in the program. By involving stakeholders in the evaluation, school counselors provide the opportunity for stakeholders to shape the evaluation and consequently the school counseling program, so that their information and programmatic needs are being met.

We are certain there are schools and districts nationally that have captured some of this potential and have done so by developing processes and mechanisms that incorporate the things stakeholders have to offer for their programs and services. Be in tune to colleagues in other school districts, and if you sense that they have strong relationships with stakeholders, contact these colleagues and learn how they work with their stakeholders. There is no formula for this kind of work. There are lots of possibilities, however, and we think there is a way to address this with your program.

What little writing that can be found on stakeholder involvement in the literature is largely focused on meeting the requirements of the ASCA National Model. For example, the writing is largely focused on things like how many meetings to have, membership, and the need for meeting agendas and meeting minutes (e.g., Carney, 1996; Idaho Division of Professional-Technical Education, 2010). Bardwell (2013) and Thomas (2011) addressed the importance of stakeholders in building support and community partnerships. And while they offered ideas that went beyond the mechanics of establishing and maintaining advisory councils, little was offered in how to productively work with stakeholders. And when it comes to incorporating stakeholders in one or more aspects of the school counseling program evaluation, beyond mentioning that this should be an aspect of an advisory council of an ASCA National Model program (ASCA, 2012), we could not find any ideas, suggestions, examples, or recommendations about how to effectively engage school counseling stakeholders in the evaluation of a school counseling program.

Evaluation Standards and Stakeholder Involvement

While there is little written on how to effectively engage stakeholders in the school counseling literature, there has been a good deal of work in the evaluation field on effective engagement of stakeholders. This work is embodied in the JCSEE Program Evaluation Standards (Yarbrough et al., 2010). While nearly all standards could be linked in one way or another to stakeholder involvement, the general attributes, utility and propriety, maintain standards that clearly articulate the importance of stakeholder engagement. Table 3.1 provides a selected sample of JCSEE Program Evaluation Standards that communicate the expectation for stakeholder involvement.

The central point here is to sensitize you as a school counselor and the school counseling profession to the explicit (and implicit) needs and concerns of a variety of stakeholders in the evaluation of your school counseling program. We want to increase understanding of the importance of stakeholders to the program and its evaluation, expand the representation of concepts and strategies to productively work with stakeholders currently found in the school

Table 3.1 Selected JCSEE program evaluation standards that support stakeholder involvement

U2 Attention to Stakeholders	Evaluations should devote attention to the full range of individuals and groups invested in the program and affected by its evaluation.
U3 Negotiated Purposes	Evaluation purposes should be identified and continually negotiated based on the needs of stakeholders.
U4 Explicit Values	Evaluations should clarify and specify the individual and cultural values underpinning purposes, processes, and judgments.
U5 Relevant Information	Evaluation information should serve the identified and emergent needs of stakeholders.
U7 Timely and Appropriate Communicating and Reporting	Evaluations should attend to the continuing information needs of their multiple audiences.
P1 Responsive and Inclusive Orientation	Evaluations should be responsive to stakeholders and their communities.
P3 Human Rights and Respect	Evaluations should be designed and conducted to protect human and legal rights and maintain the dignity of participants and other stakeholders.
P4 Clarity and Fairness	Evaluations should be understandable and fair in addressing stakeholder needs and purposes.

Source: From Yarbrough, D. B. et al. (2010). *The Program Evaluation Standards: A guide for evaluators and evaluation users* (3rd ed.). Thousand Oaks, CA: Corwin Press. Reproduced with permission from the Joint Committee for Standards in Educational Evaluation.

counseling literature, and thereby strengthen ASCA National Model (ASCA, 2012) programs. There is much to be gained in the evaluation by working productively with identified stakeholders.

School Counseling Stakeholders and Evaluation

As a starting point, know that the Management section of the ASCA National Model states, "Advisory councils made up of students, parents, teachers, school counselors, administrators and community members to review and make recommendations about school counseling program activities and results" (ASCA, 2012; p. xiii). Further, the ASCA National Model document specifies competencies for school counselors, several of which refer to school counseling stakeholders. In the section on school counselor competencies, the document states that school counselors should be able to seek and maintain "collaborations with stakeholders such as parents and guardians, teachers, administrators and community leaders… (ASCA, 2012; p. 148). These ideas form the basis for us in thinking about stakeholders for school counseling programs and the platform in which to expand stakeholder involvement in the evaluation.

In further thinking about stakeholders, there are likely important stakeholders that may not be as obvious, particularly given the interest that they have in your school counseling program and the consequent evaluation of the program. Thus, we recommend thinking systematically and inclusively about the school and broader community and recognize that there are a wide variety of connections that could compel consideration of some individuals and/or groups as stakeholders.

As an exercise in thinking about school counseling stakeholders, let's consider the school system. Since schools reside in school districts, educators throughout the school district could be stakeholders in your program. This could include, for example, teachers in other schools, particularly schools that receive students from your school, as these students advance through the system. The teachers in these other schools have some stake in the work you do to support the students they receive. Likewise, building administrators in these receiving schools will also have a stake in your school counseling program for similar reasons as the teachers. And parents in these schools may also have some stake in your school counseling program as students in your school, moving forward, could influence or impact their child's education in one way or another.

Further, school district administrators, such as the superintendent and the school counseling program director, will all have a stake in your school counseling program and, therefore, be interested in the program and services, and the evaluation. Certainly, the school board for the school district will have a stake in the school counseling program. Given the pressure for education reform and the need to get the most out of tight budgets, school boards will be keenly interested at various times in the quality of the school district's school counseling programs.

There are also community members and groups who could be interested and have a stake in your school counseling program. Mental health and other social service agencies and professionals that you might work with, could be among the community members that would be interested in the program and services provided at your school. The police department, juvenile justice system, and local colleges and universities all could have some interest in the school counseling program and services that you are responsible for. And of course, there could be others as well that are unique to your program and community.

Table 3.2 provides a list of possible school counseling stakeholders and rationales for their interest in the evaluation of the school counseling program and services. Stakeholders are organized as follows (See Walser & Trevisan, 2019, for another stakeholder organizational scheme.): Level 1 stakeholders are those closest to the program, including students, teachers, parents, program staff, and building administrators. Level 2 stakeholders are school district teachers, administrators, and parents. And Level 3 stakeholders are those from the community outside the school district, including the mental health and social service agencies, and the juvenile justice system.

An examination of the stakeholders and their interests indicates that in general, the closer stakeholders are to the program, the more their primary interests in the program, and therefore the evaluation, are focused on whether or

Table 3.2 School counseling program stakeholders

Level	Stakeholder	Reason(s) for interest in the evaluation of the school counseling program
1	Students	Am I able to get the help I need?
	Parents	Is my student receiving needed services?
	Teachers	Am I getting the support I need to help students in my classroom(s)?
	Program staff	What is working well? What needs improvement?
	Building administrators	Is the program operating effectively? Are teachers getting the support they need? What is the impact?
2	School district parents	What is the impact of the program?
	School district teachers	What is the impact of the program?
	School district administrators	What is the impact of the program?
3	Mental health professionals/agencies	What is the impact of the program?
	Social service agencies	What is the impact of the program?
	Other community members and agencies	What is the impact of the program?

not the program is operating effectively. Questions they might ask include "Are the program and services operating as planned?" and "Is the program operating effectively?" By implication, if the program is not operating effectively, then the questions "Why not?" and "What can be done to revise the program so that it can run effectively?" logically follow. In short, formative evaluation for these stakeholders is the evaluation of interest. Similarly, the stakeholders further away from the program tend to be more focused on whether or not the program is having an impact and whether or not the cost of the program is worth the money being spent for it. They are likely most interested in evaluation for summative purposes.

One last comment is to know that all stakeholders, regardless of how close or distant they are to actual program services, seek accountability. They all want to know that the program and services are meeting the needs of students and school building educators. Further, these stakeholders want to know that school counselors grasp this idea and continue to find ways to meet the needs of those who receive the benefits of the program. Evaluation has central importance in this effort.

BOX 3.1

Involving stakeholders will help to ensure that the evaluation is viewed with credibility and, in turn, that the results are acted on.

Models and Ideas for Working with Stakeholders on the Evaluation

The main recommendation for stakeholder involvement found in the ASCA National Model (ASCA, 2012) is that school counselors share the evaluation findings with the school counseling program advisory council. This recommendation is also found in the evaluation literature and contained in the JCSEE Program Evaluation Standards (Yarbrough et al., 2010). As we argue, however, stakeholders can have much stronger involvement in the evaluation of the school counseling program. As has been suggested, stakeholders can be involved in the evaluation processes and tasks, including (1) providing feedback for the development of a program logic model, (2) development of evaluation questions, (3) development and implementation of data collection instruments and protocols, (4) data analysis, and (5) providing feedback on evaluation results and recommendations. In short, there is no limit to the possibilities for stakeholder involvement.

Organizing stakeholders to effectively work on the evaluation is as important as the actual work. Well-organized stakeholder groups will help make the evaluation work more effective and efficient. Stakeholders will more likely feel that their involvement is valued and be confident that you, as the school counselor and facilitator of the evaluation, have a plan and that this plan is based on your experience and professional judgment.

Time, resources, and evaluation professional development needs are constraints that must be dealt with at any level of stakeholder involvement. Meetings to address evaluation tasks, not to mention your own time thinking through how best to involve stakeholders; labor to carry out the tasks; and training stakeholders regarding the conduct of evaluation are features of the work that you'll want to pay particular attention. Thus, as you plan your evaluation and incorporate the work of stakeholders, be mindful of the aforementioned constraints and develop a plan that makes sense.

We suggest there are three models for organizing the work of stakeholders. For some school counseling programs, which model to choose will be obvious. For others, some thought may be needed to make this determination, as the constraints of time, resources, and professional development must be accounted for. Each model is described below.

Model 1: Advisory Council

Perhaps the most straightforward way to organize the evaluation-oriented work of stakeholders is through the advisory council. The ASCA National Model recommends 6–20 individuals. Given the school community context, small, rural communities, for example, perhaps this configuration is sufficient for including all key stakeholders. Organizing the actual evaluation-oriented activities to be performed by the committee is a task for the school counselor.

Model 2: Ancillary Stakeholder Groups to the Advisory Council

In urban settings with large populations and diverse school communities, it may not be possible to obtain broad stakeholder representation through the advisory council by itself. In working on an evaluation in a fairly large community, Donaldson (2007) suggests up to 4 or 5 stakeholder groups with approximately 6 members each worked well to ensure broad stakeholder involvement. Expanding on this suggestion, we argue that the precise numbers are not what matters here. The central idea is to add sufficient numbers of subgroups to ensure broad stakeholder representation and to configure each group with a workable number of participants. Of course, the more subgroups, the more work will be needed to facilitate stakeholder interaction and articulate the work of each group with the advisory council. The use of ancillary groups, however, is a reasonable and common way in which to include stakeholders in a participatory and interactive manner to address the school counseling program evaluation.

Model 3: District-Wide School Counseling Program Evaluation

Some school districts may view each school counseling program as a component of a district-wide program. As such, the evaluation of each school's program would be part of a larger district evaluation effort. Representation from each school would be needed. Attention would also be needed to ensure that a district-wide evaluation in part meets stakeholder needs from your school. While a process like this could seem daunting to organize and facilitate, some efficiencies could be obtained with district school counselors working together. The district school counseling program director is likely providing some direction. And perhaps some stakeholder groups have a stake in more than one school program.

Each of the three models are presented in a straightforward manner for instructional purposes. Know that there are other possibilities that could be employed that are revisions to the models in some way. We do not advocate one over the other. Using each or some combination depends on the context in which your program resides. This includes the number and kinds of stakeholders for your program and the constraints you have to work with in developing a participatory evaluation approach that includes stakeholders. Context also includes the decision to include stakeholders in one or more components of the actual evaluation. Making determinations about the aforementioned contextual factors will provide the basis for selecting or developing the optimum organization for stakeholder involvement in the evaluation.

Recommendations

Working productively with stakeholder groups concerning your school counseling program and its evaluation can be a complex undertaking. There is no recipe for identifying the relevant stakeholder groups; how best to work with these groups, maintaining a balance that signals fairness and inclusiveness; and ensuring that stakeholder information needs will be met in the evaluation. Effective communication, strong interpersonal skills, political sensitivity, and ability to work with a variety of groups are essential professional skills that will be needed to address the complex undertaking of working productively to involve stakeholder groups in the evaluation.

We think school counselors are well positioned to productively work with different individuals and stakeholder groups in the evaluation. The education and training received to work with people in a counseling context provide school counselors with the skills and abilities essential to doing evaluation work, particularly with a participatory approach that includes stakeholder involvement. To be clear, we are not saying that things will be easier for you. What we are saying is that you, as a school counselor, have the foundation for navigating the complexity of working with a variety of individuals and groups. In some respects, you are better prepared for this aspect of evaluation than many in the field of evaluation who do evaluation work full time. We urge you to keep in touch with your professional experience, intuition, and skills as a counselor, as you work with a wide variety of individuals in the context of the school counseling evaluation.

BOX 3.2

School counselors are well positioned to effectively work with stakeholders and do good evaluation work.

Informed by the JCSEE Program Evaluation Standards (Yarbrough et al., 2010), and ideas offered in the evaluation literature, we offer the following recommendations as you work with stakeholders in the context of the evaluation of your school counseling program. In addition, we provide recommendations to ensure a culturally responsive evaluation.

General Stakeholder Recommendations

Recommendation 1

Take stock of the school and community stakeholders in your school counseling program. Determine their interest in participating in the evaluation. Based on the number of stakeholders and the way school counseling programs are viewed in the district, choose a stakeholder organizational model that will work for you.

Recommendation 2

Based on available time, and knowledge of evaluation, determine which components of the evaluation you want to involve stakeholders. In addition, determine whether professional development will be needed for stakeholders, and work with your school principal to explore possible ways to provide this training.

Some stakeholders have expertise that could be tapped for the evaluation. For example, there may be people with expertise in developing questionnaires, or skilled at interviewing parents. You will need to take stock of these possibilities and think critically about how this expertise might be incorporated. Providing input for constructing evaluation questions is a solid way for stakeholders to be involved in the evaluation (Preskill & Jones, 2009). Chapter 5 provides detail about this feature of the school counseling evaluation framework. In sum, it will take reflection on your part to determine the expertise of stakeholders, whether or not some professional development could be helpful, and how best to incorporate their involvement in aspects of the evaluation. The payoff toward valuing the evaluation results and findings by stakeholders through their engagement with the evaluation is clearly worth the consideration.

Recommendation 3

Work to maintain productive relationships with all stakeholders. Solid interpersonal skills, treating people with respect, and communicating effectively are all attributes of productive work with stakeholders in evaluation. These are also attributes that you have as a school counselor. Draw on your skills and abilities in dealing with people as you progress with the evaluation of the school counseling program.

Recommendation 4

Get to know the various stakeholder groups and work to understand their interests in the school counseling program and evaluation. This could take some time to fully understand. Multiple conversations and listening well will help you understand and appreciate their interests.

Recommendation 5

Communicate regularly and often to stakeholder groups about the evaluation. Think of the evaluation as having a beginning, middle, and end. Tailor the communication accordingly.

Recommendation 6

Given resources, it is likely that the evaluation will not be able to meet all stakeholder information needs. To address this, be clear with all stakeholders what the various interests and information needs are among stakeholders. Should some interests be prioritized over others, be upfront with everyone about this issue and the rationale for prioritization.

Recommendations for Culturally Responsive Evaluation

Recommendation 1

In working with stakeholder groups that are from different cultures, get to know them and their needs and concerns regarding the school counseling program. Listen well. And in many instances, being sensitive to culture and developing cultural competence will be essential.

Recommendation 2

Be vigilant in remaining sensitive to human rights and dignity, particularly for those from whom you wish to collect data. Investigate whether or not the school district maintains a policy with respect to collecting data from people in, or associated with, a school, and follow this policy closely. Absent a policy, seek guidance from school building or district administrators. Document how human rights will be protected, dignity maintained, and risks minimized in the evaluation.

Summary

Working with a representative group of stakeholders regarding evaluation of the program is essential for the evaluation to be seen as credible and, therefore, used in some way to improve or positively impact the program and services (Donaldson, 2007; Yarbrough et al., 2010). The ASCA National Model (ASCA, 2012) recommends the use of advisory councils made up of program stakeholders, largely to react to presentations of the evaluation findings by the school counselor. This chapter has stressed the point that stakeholders could be involved in all aspects of the evaluation, and with large numbers of stakeholders, the use of ancillary committees to the advisory council composed of additional program stakeholders is a viable means to organize their work.

Working effectively with stakeholders in the evaluation is a defining feature of evaluation. The JCSEE Program Evaluation Standards (Yarbrough et al., 2010) make clear that those responsible for evaluation must respond to stakeholder needs and concerns for the evaluation. The chapter identified three levels of stakeholders, each with different information needs concerning the evaluation. In short, each stakeholder group could advocate for a different purpose for the evaluation, ranging from evaluation to improve services to evaluation to determine impact. To this end, organizing stakeholders strategically will be essential for efficient and effective stakeholder involvement in the evaluation. This could be accomplished through the advisory council, ancillary groups to the advisory council, or district-wide committees. Context will help determine the best approach.

Evaluation requires professional skills to effectively work with a variety of people. School counselors are uniquely positioned to work productively with stakeholders. The training school counselors receive and the professional repertoire they develop through their practice, provides school counselors with a real advantage in developing and carrying out an evaluation of their program and services that is responsive to stakeholder interests. In turn, the evaluation will be seen as credible and, therefore, an evaluation that is more likely to be used to benefit the program.

References

American School Counselor Association (2012). *The ASCA National Model: A Framework for School Counseling Programs* (3rd ed.). Alexandria, VA.

Bardwell, B. (2013). Using your school counseling advisory councils to build school and community partnerships [PowerPoint slides].

Carney, F. (1996). Counseling and guidance advisory councils. *ERIC Digest.* Retrieved from ERIC database. (EDO-CG-96-25).

Donaldson, S. I. (2007). *Program theory-driven evaluation science: Strategies and applications.* New York, NY: Psychology Press Taylor & Francis Group.

Idaho Division of Professional-Technical Education (2010). School counseling program handbook for advisory councils.

Preskill, H. & Jones, N. (2009). *A practical guide for engaging stakeholders in developing evaluation questions.* Robert Wood Johnson Foundation Evaluation Series.

Thomas, S. W. (2011). The impact of a comprehensive school counseling plan (*Counselor Education Master's Theses*). The College at Brockport, State University of New York.

Walser, T. M. & Trevisan, M. S. (2019). Completing your evaluation dissertation, (*Thesis, or final project*). Los Angeles, CA: Sage. Manuscript under review.

Yarbrough, D. B., Shulha, L. M., Hopson, R. K., & Caruthers, F. A. (2010). *The Program Evaluation Standards: A guide for evaluators and evaluation users* (3rd ed.). Thousand Oaks, CA: Corwin Press.

4 Developing Theories of Action and Logic Models

Questions to Consider

- What are the benefits associated with creating a theory of action and associated logic model for a school counseling program?
- How are logic models used in formative and summative evaluation?
- What are the advantages of including a logic model in an action plan?
- How can a logic model improve the alignment of activities and desired outcomes?
- How does a logic model guide program evaluation?
- How are logic models developed?
- What considerations are necessary for using logic models in formative and summative evaluation?
- What considerations are necessary for the proper use of logic models in culturally responsive evaluations?

Vignette

Lijuan is a counselor in a K–8 elementary school. The fourth and fifth grade teachers asked her for help because some of their students needed additional support to become more academically motivated, planful, and independent in their schoolwork. She searched the internet and school counseling journals to find a *small-group curriculum* that fit with the expressed needs of the teacher. She found True Goals, a goal-setting curriculum that was well-documented, appropriate for the ages of the students, and seemingly aligned with the goals established by the teacher. **She drafted a logic model** that identified (1) the resources (inputs) she would need to implement True Goals, (2) the foci of the major clusters of the True Goal curriculum (activities), (3) the things that participating students should know and be able to do immediately after participation (outputs), (4) the changes in school behavior that would be expected in the weeks immediately after True Goals participation (proximal outcomes), and (5) the long-term expected benefits to students (distal outcomes). **The teachers reviewed the logic model** and endorsed her use of True Goals. **Lijuan also shared the logic model with the principal and assistant principal** who approved her proposed small-group format and provided the resources she needed for the group. Lijuan **used the logic model to develop a plan for a formative evaluation** of her True Goals implementation. Lijuan *documented all this information in her ASCA National Model action plan* (ASCA, 2012).

The ASCA National Model and Action Plans

In order to ensure that useful information will be generated for program improvement and accountability, program evaluations should be planned at the same time as programs are designed and program activities are developed or selected. The ASCA National Model (ASCA, 2012) recognizes the importance of integrating program evaluation and planning the activities of the school counseling program, and it uses action plans to accomplish this integration. Action plans are developed for curriculum-based, closing-the-gap, and small-group activities. An action plan includes a detailed description of the goals, content, and implementation of the activity. An action plan also includes a description of the expected benefits for students, how the activity will be evaluated, and how results will be communicated to stakeholders. The ASCA National Model requires that a similar process be used for ensuring the integration of program evaluation with lesson plans.

Program Theory Evaluation

Program theory evaluation (Sharpe, 2011) is an approach to program evaluation that maps the logic underlying a program and its activities and tests whether or not desired results are being attained. Like the use of action plans, program theory evaluation helps to ensure that program evaluation results in useful knowledge and that the program activities are carefully planned and considered beforehand. The use of program theory evaluation, however, has several additional important features including its focus on (1) clearly specifying the resources needed for successful implementation beforehand, (2) ensuring the alignment of activities with desired benefits, (3) ensuring that all program staff share a common understanding of program activities and expected benefits, (4) identifying the relationships between short-term changes resulting from an activity and long-term expected benefits, and (5) providing guidance for both formative and summative program evaluations. In addition, program theory evaluation is flexible and is useful in design and evaluation of whole programs in addition to program activities. In program theory evaluation, theories of action and logic models are used to assist both program planning and evaluation. Given these advantages, we advocate using theories of action and logic models in the generation of school counseling action plans and in the evaluation of the school counseling program as a whole.

BOX 4.1

Theories of action and associated logic models are powerful tools that support program design, monitoring, and evaluation.

Theories of Action and Logic Models

A theory of action is a description of the logic underlying the operation of a program (Patton 1978). A theory of action is generated to ensure that all the *implicit* assumptions and beliefs about a program are made *explicit* so that they can be examined, verified, and evaluated. It is important to have an explicit description of important features such as the resources that are needed to support program activities, the relationships among the components of the program, the relationship between activities and expected benefits, and the relationships between the immediate outcomes of program activities and the long-term benefits that are expected to result from participation in the program.

Constructing a theory of action is best done as a component of program planning, as the program is being developed or as a new program activity is being designed. It is best done collaboratively with the involvement of stakeholders so that any differences in assumptions or understandings can be surfaced and reconciled. Once a good theory of action is developed, a program evaluation can be designed that "tests" the explicit contentions.

Developing a logic model is the most common way to generate a theory of action. A logic model is a graphic representation of a theory of action that includes the essential components of the program and the hypothesized relationships among these components.

There are many formats for constructing logic models. The approach described here is derived from Frechtling (2007), Dimmitt, Carey, and Hatch (2007), and Martin and Carey (2014).

A logic model has four basic components: (1) inputs, (2) activities, (3) outputs, and (4) outcomes. It is often useful to identify two types of outcomes, proximal outcomes and distal outcomes. Inputs include all the resources that are necessary for the effective delivery of program activities. These resources might include items such as school counselor planning time to develop an activity, counselor time needed to deliver the activity, curriculum materials that need to be purchased, and training that is needed for effective implementation of the activity.

Activities are the active agents of the program that are intended to result in learning and change and result in benefits for students. School counseling activities can include direct services such as one-on-one counseling sessions, guidance lessons, and curriculum-based, closing-the-gap, and small-group interventions. School counseling activities can also include indirect services such as parent training, parent consultation, teacher consultation, and advocacy.

Outputs are the changes that are expected to occur immediately after the activity. From an evaluation perspective, outputs can be thought of as the immediate evidence that the activity has had an effect. For example, after a training activity in goal setting, students should be able to describe the characteristics of a good goal and formulate good goals for themselves. After a parent education group, parents can be expected to identify different styles of parenting and the advantages and disadvantages of each.

Outcomes are the long-term changes that are expected to result as a consequence of participation in the activity. Students who learn goal setting can be expected to manage their time (proximal outcome), which will in turn result in enhanced academic achievement (distal outcome). Parents who actively participate in a parenting skills class can be expected to use more democratic parenting approaches at home (proximal outcome) that will result in their children developing higher levels of self-direction and intrinsic motivation (distal outcome). Figure 4.1 contains a simple logic model for True Goals (Martin, 2015), a school counselor–designed curriculum to teach effective goal setting in small-group format.

An effective implementation of True Goals requires a manual and workbook for every student; approximately 6 hours of self-study time to learn how to implement the group lessons; the establishment of a group pre-selection process that ensures that the students who are selected for the group need and are likely to benefit from learning goal setting; and time to lead 10 weekly, 30-minute group sessions. True Goals activities cluster in three foci: (1) helping students learn the characteristics of good goals, (2) helping students apply the goal-setting process to their own lives, and (3) helping students use the goal-setting process to achieve a balance between academic achievement–related goals and social goals. If students learn the intended lessons, they should be able to write good goals, develop meaningful personal goals for themselves, and write achievement goals in addition to social goals. In the short-term, this learning is expected to result in higher levels of self-directed behavior and higher levels of intrinsically motivated self-regulated learning. These in turn are expected to be reflected in a higher level of well-being associated with having a sense of agency and higher levels of academic achievement.

Utility of Logic Models

Logic models have some uses and advantages that argue for their inclusion in action planning. Developing a logic model ensures that the program or activity is well considered, that everyone involved knows exactly what will be done and why, the needed resources are identified, and there is alignment among the expected long-term benefits and the specific activities.

Logic models also have wonderful communicative value. They are a great way to help decision-makers and other stakeholders understand the inner workings of a program or a program activity and the associated resource needs and expected benefits. During the planning process, stakeholders should be

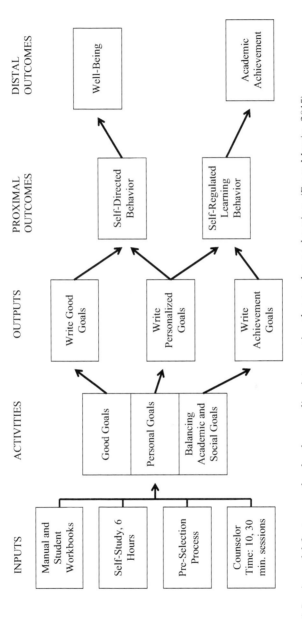

Figure 4.1 Logic model for true goals school counseling intervention that teaches goal setting. (From Martin, 2015)

involved in the development of the logic model, especially in the specification of the proximal outcomes and distal outcomes. Stakeholders can weigh in on the short-term knowledge growth and long-term expected benefits and behavioral changes that should be expected from the program or activity. A good logic model ensures that parents, school administrators, school counselors, and students share a common understanding of, and agreement with, the goals and benefits of the program or activity.

Logic models also help to focus program evaluations by clearly specifying the hypotheses that need to be tested in formative and summative evaluations.

BOX 4.2

Logic models are helpful tools for ensuring that all stakeholder groups understand and agree with the design of a program or intervention.

Logic Models and Formative Evaluation

Formative evaluations involve testing the hypothesized relationships between inputs, activities, and outputs. Such formative evaluations ask questions like,

- Are the activities being delivered fully and with fidelity?
- Are the resources sufficient to support the delivery of the activities?
- Are participants learning what is intended from the activities?

Answering these types of formative evaluation questions can guide the improvement of the activities themselves and improvement in how the activities are delivered. Improving the implementation of the activities through formative evaluation increases their potency and their ability to produce their intended benefits. There is no point in conducting a summative evaluation until there is evidence that the activities have potency.

Logic Models and Summative Evaluation

Summative evaluations involve testing the hypothesized relationships between the activities and the proximal and distal outcomes. Such summative evaluations ask questions like,

- Do participants in the activities show positive changes in school-related behavior?
- Do participants in the activities receive the intended long-term benefits?
- Does participation in the activities result in any unexpected harm?

Answering these types of summative evaluation questions can guide the assessment of impact and contribute to an assessment of the value and worth of the activities. Dimmitt, Carey, and Hatch (2007) have noted that it is most often advisable to focus summative evaluations of school counseling specific activities and interventions on the proximal outcomes because of statistical power considerations. Given the relatively small number of participants typically involved in the evaluation (and the number of additional factors affecting the distal outcomes), evaluations focusing on proximal outcomes are usually more sensitive tests of effectiveness of a specific activity or intervention. In Chapter 7 we will discuss the measurement of proximal outcomes.

Developing a Logic Model for a Specific Activity or Intervention

Logic models are best developed during planning and with the involvement of stakeholders. In these cases, they are typically developed in a "backward" fashion, starting with the specification of the desired distal outcomes, the long-term changes that are desired by stakeholders. Next, the proximal outcomes are added. These represent the desired changes in student behavior that are expected to result in the distal outcomes.

Then, activities that align with the proximal outcomes are either developed or selected and the outputs that reflect the immediate learning associated with each activity that is predictive of attainment of each proximal outcome are added. Finally, the resources needed for effective implementation of the activities are added. This "backward" design method ensures alignment of the activities, outputs, and outcomes.

Logic models are also useful to map already-existing activities and programs to develop a common understanding among implementers and stakeholders and to plan formative and summative program evaluations. In this case, different stakeholder may be asked to independently map the program's logic and the different maps can be compared and integrated. The inputs and activities identified by this process must be confirmed by the program evaluation. The outputs and outcomes reflect the things that need to be measured by program evaluations.

A Logic Model for an ASCA National Model Program

Theories of action and associated logic models can be used to describe the inner workings of the whole program in addition to the specific activities and interventions within a program. The ASCA National Model (ASCA, 2006) was not developed using a program theory-based approach to program design. It was originally developed in the late 1990s as a political response to perceived threats to the school counseling profession resultant from widespread adoption of standards-based models of education across the US. The ASCA National Model was developed through a blending of Comprehensive Developmental Guidance (Gysbers & Henderson, 1988), Developmental Guidance and Counseling (Myrick, 1987), and Results-Based Guidance (Johnson & Johnson

1991), to create a common program model that would include the essential elements of the three existing models and that would align the school counseling program with the principles and practices of standards-based education. Many school counselors felt threatened by standards-based educational reform because it focused almost exclusively on the goal of promoting academic achievement (as opposed to more traditional counseling goals such as vocational choice, college placement, social skills development, self-knowledge development, and mental health). In addition, ASCA sought to create a unified model to eliminate competition among proponents of the three traditional models. Both the alignment with standards-based education and the creation of a unified model for the school counseling program were seen as necessary responses to a climate that was perceived as threatening to school counselors and the profession. The current third-edition ASCA National Model (ASCA, 2012) retains all of the essential features of the original model.

Martin and Carey (2014) developed a retrospective logic model to guide evaluation of ASCA National Model programs (see Figure 4.2). They analyzed the ASCA National Model (ASCA, 2012) and ancillary documents explicating the Model and extracted a series of "if-then" statements from which the Model's underlying theory could be inferred.

Their analysis suggests that the ASCA National Model is intended to achieve three major programmatic outcomes: (1) increased student achievement and associated reductions in achievement gaps, (2) systemic change and school improvement, and (3) increased program resources. Summative evaluations of ASCA National Model programs should measure all three of these desired outcomes in order to gauge the level of success of the program.

Martin and Carey's (2014) analysis indicates that there are six types of activities that are performed in ASCA National Model programs: (1) direct services, (2) indirect services, (3) school counselor personnel evaluation, (4) program management processes, (5) program evaluation, and (6) program advocacy. Each of these activities has associated outputs (that are in turn related to one or more outcomes). Formative evaluations of ASCA National Model programs should examine whether or not the activities are being performed properly and, if so, whether or not the expected outputs do indeed result from the activities. For example, indirect service activities (e.g., consultation and school leadership) are hypothesized to result in positive student change, increased parent involvement, increased teacher competence, and better school polices and processes. If an output does not result from its associated activities, redesign of the activities is needed.

Furthermore, Martin and Carey's (2014) analysis indicates that successful implementation of an ASCA National Model program is dependent on the model's foundational elements (e.g., vision statement) and having adequate program resources (e.g., adequate number of school counselors and appropriate use of school counselor time). Again, formative evaluations need to assess whether or not the foundational elements are in place and whether or not adequate resources are available to support the conduct of the program's activities.

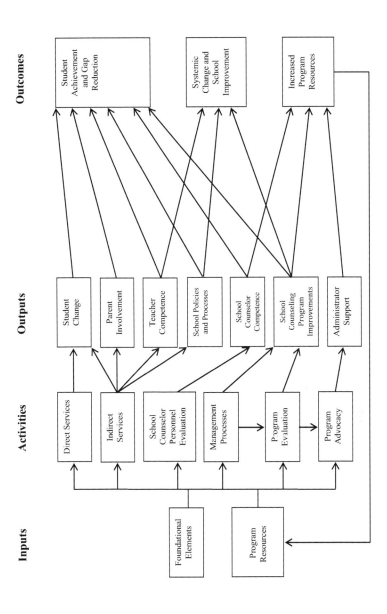

Figure 4.2 Logic model for ASCA National Model School Counseling Programs. (From "Development of a logic model to guide evaluations of the ASCA National Model for School Counseling Programs," by I. Martin and J. C. Carey, 2014, *The Professional Counselor*, 4, p. 462. Copyright 2014 by the National Board for Certified Counselors, Inc. and Affiliates. Reproduced with permission.)

BOX 4.3

Logic models guide the formative and summative evaluation of whole school counseling programs and the elements of these programs.

Evaluation Standards and Theories of Action

While you won't find the words "program theory" or "logic model" in the JCSEE Program Evaluation Standards or associated standards statements (Yarbrough et al., 2010), there is a strong and broad connection to JCSEE Program Evaluation Standards, particularly the utility, feasibility, propriety, and accuracy standards (Trevisan & Walser, 2015; p. 64). Since program theory is best developed with stakeholder input, any of the JCSEE Utility standards that address stakeholder involvement and their needs and concerns connects well and supports school counseling program theory. In addition, a logic model can incorporate a variety of programmatic transactions in order to implement activities and achieve outcomes (see Figure 4.2). Thus, feasibility standards that address practicality and context support program theory and logic models. Moreover, nearly all of the accuracy standards support program theory and logic models (e.g., valid and reliable information, explicit program and context statements). And, the expectation for thorough evaluation documentation found in the accountability standards supports the development of program theory and logic models. Table 4.1 provides a sample of some of the JCSEE Program Evaluation Standards (Yarbrough et al., 2010) that connect and support program theory and logic models for the conduct of high-quality evaluation work.

Logic Modeling and Culturally Responsive Evaluation

Many of the schools in the US are multicultural organizations where the majority of the staff belong to different racial/ethnic and socioeconomic groups

Table 4.1 Selected JCSEE program evaluation standards that support theories of action

U2 Attention to Stakeholders	Evaluations should devote attention to the full range of individuals and groups invested in the program and affected by its evaluation.
F2 Practical Procedures	Evaluation procedures should be practical and responsive to the way the program operates.
A4 Explicit Program and Context Descriptions	Evaluations should document programs and their contexts with appropriate detail and scope for the evaluation purposes.
E1 Evaluation Documentation	Evaluations should fully document their negotiated purposes and implemented designs, procedures, data, and outcomes.

Source: From Yarbrough, D. B. et al. (2010). *The Program Evaluation Standards: A guide for evaluators and evaluation users* (3rd ed.). Thousand Oaks, CA: Corwin Press. Reproduced with permission from the Joint Committee for Standards in Educational Evaluation.

than the majority of students and families. Programs, interventions, and their associated evaluations need to be grounded within the cultural context in which the program or intervention takes place and need to be appropriate for the culture(s) of the target group(s). This is true for theories of action and the associated logic models.

Trevisan and Carey (2020) have identified some best practices in logic model development in multicultural contexts. They suggest that in multicultural contexts, extensive stakeholder involvement by representative members of the school's communities in logic model development is of paramount importance to make sure that there is consonance between the beliefs, expectations, and goals of the implementers and the recipients of services. Furthermore, they suggest that the cultural competence of program implementers needs to be explicitly included as an essential element of the inputs of the logic model and needs to be evaluated as part of any formative evaluation. Evaluations need to test whether or not the school counselors themselves possess sufficient cultural competence to effectively implement the program or activity with the school's diverse groups. Finally, they suggest that in all situations when an existing program or activity has not been grounded in the cultural context of the stakeholders (the logic model has not been adequately vetted and/or the cultural competence of the implementers is not adequately considered in the logic model and program), evaluations need to determine the extent to which this lack of grounding is affecting the ability of the program to achieve its goals. In these instances, evaluation also needs to suggest ways to address the limitations that result from the lack of consonance between program staff and program clients.

Summary

The many advantages of program theory evaluation argue for the use of theories of action and logic modeling in the generation of school counseling action plans and in the evaluation of the school counseling program as a whole. Logic models represent a pictorial summary of a theory of action. They are useful in program planning, communicating the goals and inner workings of a program to decision-makers, and guiding formative and summative program evaluations. Logic models can be used with the whole program or with the constituent activities or interventions of a program. In multicultural contexts, special care must be taken to assure broad input from all stakeholder groups and to identify the cultural competencies of counselors that are necessary for effective delivery of program services.

References

American School Counselor Association. (2006). *The ASCA national model: A framework for school counseling programs* (2nd ed.). Alexandria, VA: Author.

American School Counselor Association. (2012). *The ASCA national model: A framework for school counseling programs* (3rd ed.). Alexandria, VA: Author.

Dimmitt, C., Carey, J., & Hatch, T. (2007). *Evidence-based school counseling: Making a difference with data-driven practices.* New York, NY: Corwin Press.

Frechtling, J. A. (2007). *Logic modeling methods in program evaluation.* New York, NY: Wiley & Sons.

Gysbers, N. & Henderson, P. (1988). *Developing and managing your school guidance program.* Alexandria, VA: American Association for Counseling and Development.

Johnson, S. K. & Johnson, C. D. (1991). The new guidance: A systems approach to pupil personnel programs. *California Association of Counseling and Development,* 11, 5–14.

Martin, I. (2015). *True Goals: A school counseling curriculum.* San Diego, CA: Swallowtail Educational Consulting.

Martin, I. & Carey, J. C. (2014). Development of a logic model to guide evaluations of the ASCA National Model for School Counseling Programs. *The Professional Counselor,* 4, 455–466.

Myrick, R. D. (1987) *Developmental guidance and counseling: A practical approach.* Minneapolis, IN: Educational Medial Corporation.

Patton, M. Q. (1978). *Utilization-focused evaluation.* Beverly Hills, CA: Sage.

Sharpe, G. (2011). A review of program theory and theory-based evaluations. *American International Journal of Contemporary Research,* 1, 72–75.

Trevisan, M. S. & Carey, J. C. (2020). Evaluating intercultural programs and interventions. In A. Portera, R. Moodley & M. Milani (Eds.), *Intercultural mediation, counselling and psychotherapy in Europe.* Cambridge, UK: Cambridge Scholars.

Trevisan, M. S. & Walser, T. M. (2015). *Evaluability assessment: Improving evaluation quality and use.* Los Angeles, CA: Sage.

Yarbrough, D. B., Shulha, L. M., Hopson, R. K., & Caruthers, F. A. (2010). *The Program Evaluation Standards: A guide for evaluators and evaluation users* (3rd ed.). Thousand Oaks, CA: Corwin Press.

5   Developing School Counseling Program Evaluation Questions

Questions to Consider

- What are evaluation questions and what are the benefits for developing evaluation questions?
- What evaluation questions focus on formative evaluation?
- What evaluation questions focus on summative evaluation?
- What are the consequences of poor or no evaluation questions?
- What evaluations questions do you think different school counseling stakeholders will be interested in?
- Reflect on your own skills in working with people. What approach would you take in obtaining school counseling stakeholder input for developing evaluation questions? Where do you see the possibility for difficulties in the process and how would you handle them?
- If achieving consensus for evaluation questions among stakeholders is difficult in a particular evaluation, how might you as a school counselor handle this situation?

Vignette

Jerry is a school counselor at Mountain View High School. The high school faces many student and family challenges that can impact negatively on teaching and learning. Bullying, depression, and suicide occur at a high rate among students. A high percentage of families are low income, with many below the poverty line. In addition, the school's population is diverse, with many different ethnic and racial groups. A significant proportion of the population includes recent immigrants to the US, and thus, learning English is critical for most of the immigrant students.

To help deal with these student and family challenges, Jerry worked with his school counseling colleagues to *implement the ASCA National Model* (ASCA, 2012) to organize its school counseling program and services. As a consequence, *an advisory council has been established in the school* with representation from key stakeholder groups. Jerry considers **broad stakeholder input into the** evaluation of the school counseling program as crucial to the viability of the evaluation and believes that he can achieve a good deal of support for the program from their involvement. He views **broad stakeholder input as a form of accountability**, ensuring that the school counseling program responds to the needs and concerns of stakeholders. As a consequence, Jerry believes **that stakeholders will deepen their support for the school counseling program** if they see that their needs and concerns are being met. Some will become strong advocates.

Jerry works with the school's advisory council to generate a broad list of evaluation questions for the school counseling program. This is an important initial step in the evaluation process as the evaluation questions set the direction for the evaluation tasks and activities. The list is reviewed by the advisory council. The goal with the review is to pare the list to a manageable number of evaluation questions that the evaluation could address, given time and resources. If necessary, another round of review and feedback is conducted, and this process is repeated until a viable list of questions is agreed upon. This process is used for each evaluation.

The Importance of Sound Evaluation Questions

Evaluation questions are the starting point for developing your school counseling program evaluation. Evaluation questions build on the program logic model by explicating program components and processes and putting them under the evaluation spotlight. As several authors have suggested over many years, evaluation questions set the focus and direction for the evaluation (e.g., Cronbach, 1982; Fitzpatrick, Sanders, & Worthen, 2011; Preskill & Jones, 2009). Preskill and Jones (2009) indicate that good evaluation questions

- Establish the boundary and scope of an evaluation and communicate to others what the evaluation will and will not address.
- Are the broad, overarching questions that the evaluation will seek to answer; they are not survey or interview questions.
- Reflect diverse perspectives and experiences.
- Are aligned with clearly articulated goals and objectives.
- Can be answered through data collection and analysis. (p. 8)

Evaluation questions are best developed with broad stakeholder input. While stakeholders typically don't formulate the precise questions, at least initially, they inform their development. The benefits are numerous. Broad stakeholder input into the development of evaluation questions helps to ensure that the questions are relevant, credible, and useful (Preskill & Jones, 2009). Stakeholder input will help to ensure that their needs and concerns for evaluation information are met. In turn, the evaluation will more likely be used for "learning, decision-making, and taking action" (Preskill & Jones, 2009; p. 6), the ultimate aim of all evaluations. Recall the ideas presented in Chapter 3 on ways to work with stakeholders in developing and carrying out the evaluation of your school counseling program. As you progress with this chapter, consider these ideas in working with stakeholders for developing evaluation questions. Again, evaluation questions set the stage for the remainder of the evaluation work. Stakeholder involvement in developing these questions forms the basis of a credible evaluation of your school counseling program.

BOX 5.1

Evaluation questions are best developed with broad stakeholder input.

Evaluation Standards and Evaluation Questions

The JCSEE Program Evaluation Standards (Yarbrough et al., 2010) speak to the importance of stakeholder involvement in evaluation processes and, by implication, development of evaluation questions. Many of the standards listed in Chapter 3 pertain to stakeholder involvement for evaluation questions, particularly the utility standards. Please refer to Chapter 3 to refresh your memory about these specific standards. In addition, Table 5.1 provides selected JCSEE Program Evaluation Standards that speak to the importance of clear and appropriate evaluation questions.

Table 5.1 Selected JCSEE Program Evaluation Standards that Support Evaluation Questions

A1 Justified Conclusions and Decisions	Evaluation conclusions and decisions should be explicitly justified in the cultures and contexts where they have consequences.
A2 Valid Information	Evaluation information should serve the intended purposes and support valid interpretations.
A3 Reliable Information	Evaluation procedures should yield sufficiently dependable and consistent information for the intended uses.
A6 Sound Design and Analyses	Evaluations should employ technically adequate designs and analyses that are appropriate for the evaluation purposes.
A7 Explicit Evaluation Reasoning	Evaluation reasoning leading from information and analyses to findings, interpretations, conclusions, and judgments should be clearly and completely documented.
E1 Evaluation Documentation	Evaluations should fully document their negotiated purposes and implemented designs, procedures, data, and outcomes.

Source: From Yarbrough, D. B (2010). *The Program Evaluation Standards: A guide for evaluators and evaluation users* (3rd ed.). Thousand Oaks, CA: Corwin Press. Reproduced with permission from the Joint Committee for Standards in Educational Evaluation.

All of the above standards point to the importance of starting with clear, consistent, and sound evaluation questions. All subsequent evaluation tasks and activities fall out from the evaluation questions. More specifically, the aforementioned evaluation standards point to evaluation questions that will set the direction for selection of methods, data collection and analysis, development of findings, and recommendations. In sum, the evaluation standards communicate by implication the importance and centrality of evaluation questions to effective evaluation.

Formulating a Workable Set of Evaluation Questions

There are lots of ways to formulate evaluation questions. Typically, this entails connecting evaluation questions to an organizing framework. As a means to illuminate the purposes of formative and summative evaluation, Chapter 1 indicated the types of things the evaluation would focus on for each purpose: program improvement for formative evaluation and assessment of impact for summative evaluation. The chapter depicted more direction for the evaluation by alluding to evaluation questions. For formative evaluation, logical questions include, "What is working well?" and "What needs improvement?" And for summative evaluation, logical questions include, "Did the program have intended impact?" Thus, evaluation questions could reasonably be organized by the purpose for the evaluation.

Chapter 4 provided an additional means to stimulate thinking about evaluation questions by connecting the questions to the logic model for the program. A sample of questions was provided. Given the strong need and benefit of developing a logic model for the school counseling program, we argue that the logic model likely provides the most productive and useful means to organize and develop evaluation questions. The benefits are compelling. One, developing evaluation questions based on the logic model connects these two components of the school counseling evaluation framework. There is a certain efficiency to this connection, and it also provides further clarity for stakeholders interested in the evaluation. Two, by developing evaluation questions in response to the program logic model, evaluation questions are grounded in salient aspects of the program. In short, the program and its evaluation are woven together almost seamlessly. Recall that a logic model has four components: (1) inputs, (2) activities, (3) outputs, and (4) outcomes. Evaluation questions can then be generated and organized by considering each component.

There are many processes that could be used to develop a workable set of evaluation questions, a set of questions that can be addressed in the timeframe specified, and the resources allotted for the evaluation tasks and activities. The core of these processes is a kind of back-and-forth between stakeholder ideas and those in charge of culling the information provided and presenting it back to stakeholders for another look. Cronbach (1982) referred to this process as having a divergent and convergent phase. The divergent phase entails the development of broad lists of ideas for evaluation questions. Often these ideas are not actually in the form of evaluation questions but signal evaluation questions in one way or another. The convergent phase works to cull through the broad list and (1) revise the ideas presented into evaluation questions, (2) eliminate redundancies, and (3) begin to prioritize the list with a view toward a workable set. This process could take several iterations. In short, the general idea is to generate a list in each stakeholder committee or subcommittee, submit the list to the school counselors in charge of the evaluation, and, once the list has been reviewed and revised, send the list back out to committees for further review.

When the list of evaluation questions is sent back to subcommittees, it will be important to explain to stakeholders present how and why a particular idea was revised. In addition, if some evaluation questions are prioritized over others, an explanation as to why will also be important. By providing explanations of changes to ideas generated, a form of evaluation education occurs, generating evaluation capacity among stakeholders. With greater understanding about evaluation, stakeholders will be in a better position to inform and support the evaluation. And by providing rationale for revision and prioritization, there is transparency and accountability in the process. Individual stakeholders will see "what happened" to their idea presented after review and revision. And last, be flexible. Discussion, negotiation, and compromise could be needed to finalize a workable list of evaluation questions.

Sample Evaluation Questions

Table 5.2 provides a list of sample evaluation questions that could logically be developed and used within the context of your school counseling program evaluation. Each evaluation question is categorized based on the program logic model component. Note that in some cases, there could be more than one logic model component to the categorization for a particular evaluation question.

Considerations in Working with Stakeholders to Develop Evaluation Questions

The aforementioned ideas will help you as a school counselor to work productively with stakeholders to develop sound evaluation questions. In turn, the foundation for a productive evaluation of your school counseling program will have been laid. Of course, the process of the evaluation that includes development of instruments, data collection, data analysis, and recommendations must all be done productively for the best evaluation outcome. The importance of evaluation questions to the evaluation must be emphasized here, as it is the starting point for the development of instructions, data collection, data analysis, and recommendations.

The aforementioned benefits are clear. The consequences of poorly constructed evaluation questions, however, are also noteworthy, and school counselors should be cognizant of these negative possibilities. In a well-respected

Table 5.2 Sample evaluation questions by logic model component

Logic model component	Evaluation question

Inputs	Are resources deployed as planned?
	    Counselor planning time?
	    Counselor time to deliver activities?
	    Counselor training to deliver program?
	    Program budget?

	Are the resources being used efficiently?
	    Counselor planning time?
	    Counselor time to deliver activities?
	    Counselor training to deliver program?
	    Program budget?

	Is the cost for the school counseling program reasonable in relation to the proposed benefits?
Activities	What component(s) of the school counseling program is working well?
	What needs improvement?
	Are the intended prevention, social emotional, and other curricula being delivered with high fidelity to the intended students?
	Are some students affected more by the school counseling program than others?
	Does the school counseling program work better under some conditions than others?
	Are indirect services (e.g., consultation, referrals, collaboration) responsive to the needs of students and teachers?
	Are external agencies and other resources being utilized in an optimum way?
	Would alternative educational approaches (as part of the direct service component of the school counseling program) yield equivalent or more benefits at less cost?
Outputs	How many students received the intervention?
	How many teachers participated?
	Are the planned short-term changes being achieved?
Outcomes	Are the long-term or ultimate outcomes being achieved?
	Does the school counseling program have any unintended consequences?
	Are there students with needs that the school counseling program is not reaching?

evaluation text, the authors specify the consequences of poorly constructed evaluation questions this way:

- Little or no payoff from the expenditure for the evaluation.
- A myopic evaluation focus that misdirects future efforts
- Loss of goodwill or credibility because an audience's important questions or concerns are omitted.

- Disenfranchisement of legitimate stakeholders.
- Unjustified conclusions. (Fitzpatrick, Sanders, & Worthen, 2011; p. 246)

Poorly constructed evaluation questions have the potential to stymie or derail your work despite the best of intentions for the evaluation of your school counseling program. Thus, clearly thinking through and implementing a plan for working with stakeholders concerning evaluation questions is foundational to developing sound evaluation questions as well as to the overall success of the evaluation.

The process of working with stakeholders in the development of evaluation questions can also stimulate thinking and learning about what is possible in the evaluation of the school counseling program. As mentioned in Chapter 3, when considering the evaluation of the school counseling program, school administrators likely want to know if the program is having an impact. Teachers on the other hand, will likely focus on whether or not they are getting the support they need from the school counseling program in order to provide effective instruction to their students. Different data are needed to address the concerns of these two stakeholder groups. Depending on time and resources, a decision could be required to collect data to address one group's concerns and not the other.

Donaldson (2007) indicates that in the development of evaluation questions and the subsequent plan, stakeholders will begin to see the difference in data collection strategies between formative and summative evaluation. Formative evaluation typically uses a good deal of interviews, questionnaires, and observations. These methods are typically not up to the demands of providing valid evidence for impact, the kind of impact evidence ultimately envisioned by ASCA (2012) or impact evidence that will resonate with decision-makers. What can occur is that stakeholders experience the conflict between information collected that is suitable for formative evaluation and evidence for impact. In short, the same methods cannot be used for both formative and summative evaluation purposes.

The distinction and sometimes conflict between formative and summative evaluation can also move to a focus on the credibility of the evaluation evidence for either purpose as well as the resource constraints that are always present when conducting evaluation. Stakeholders could, for example, become energized by the possibilities offered through evaluation, only to become discouraged once they realize what is required to obtain strong evidence for impact.

There is no fully accepted or failsafe strategy for dealing with conflicts among stakeholders for answering various evaluation questions. Donaldson (2007) maintains that the best that can be done when competing priorities in evaluation questions are present in an evaluation is to gauge for stakeholders the cost and feasibility of answering evaluation questions. In turn, difficult decisions can become more obvious for stakeholders, once they know the resources that are required to answer these questions.

We think there is another approach that dovetails with your strengths as a school counselor. In the spirit of compromise, an evaluation one year might focus on formative evaluation while an evaluation in a subsequent year might focus on summative evaluation. A bit of creativity and flexibility could go a long way in smoothing tensions when competing ideas for priority evaluation questions are voiced. Most, if not all, evaluation questions concerning the school counseling program could then be addressed. And remember, as we've made the case in previous chapters, you are well positioned as a school counselor to address conflict, differences of opinion, and foster compromise. The training you received as a school counselor, and the predilection and skillset to work with a variety of people, has prepared you for this part of evaluation work. Keep in touch with your professional strengths as you work with school counseling evaluation stakeholders.

Capacity building among stakeholders about the program and the evaluation is a possible, and important, positive outcome in engaging stakeholders in the development of evaluation questions (Donaldson, 2007). Stakeholders learn more detail about the inner workings of a program than previously known, see what is needed to improve program components, understand the importance of evaluation to the overall impact of the school counseling program, and learn how to develop an evaluation that responds to the school counseling program. The capacity building potential for involving stakeholders in the development of evaluation questions is perhaps one of the greatest benefits to the school counseling program.

Evaluation Questions and Culturally Responsive Evaluation

As should be apparent, involving broad stakeholders in any aspect of the evaluation is a solid means to foster a culturally responsive evaluation. Thus, the recommendations for a culturally responsive evaluation detailed in Chapter 3 also apply to the development of evaluation questions. In addition, evaluation questions signal the kinds of data collection strategies that will be needed. Depending on the question, some data collection methods could be strategies that resonate strongly with different cultural groups; that is, these groups could view these methods as more valid than other strategies. Interviews, for example, by individuals from the particular cultural group, is an example of such a strategy (Trevisan & Carey, 2020). Moreover, the evaluation questions not only signal particular data collection methods, but also signal reporting strategies that could be viewed as more valid and meaningful than other strategies. Perhaps the most obvious is reporting about aspects of the evaluation in the language of a particular cultural group. In sum, the development of evaluation questions in a culturally responsive manner includes (1) developing questions that are important to key cultural groups, (2) anticipating methods that are viewed as valid by these groups, and (3) further anticipating reporting strategies that will reach these groups in a way that is meaningful (AEA, 2011).

BOX 5.2

Clearly thinking through and implementing a plan for working with stakeholders to construct evaluation questions is foundational to developing sound evaluation questions as well as to the overall success of the evaluation.

Summary

The benefits of developing sound evaluation questions toward high expectations for a credible and useful evaluation have been addressed in this chapter. Working closely with school counseling stakeholders in developing evaluation questions is the surest way of achieving these expectations, and the JSCEE Program Evaluation Standards (Yarbrough et al., 2010) embody this thinking. Organizing the development of evaluation questions by using the logic model connects two components of the school counseling evaluation framework, fostering efficiency and greater understanding for the evaluation. Moreover, by including stakeholders, a culturally responsive evaluation can be achieved, one that responds to the needs and concerns of cultural groups within the school counseling community. In addition, the development of evaluation questions with the involvement of stakeholders provides an opportunity for evaluation capacity building among a wide variety of school counseling stakeholders, both within the school and district, and in the community. Given the knowledge and skills of school counselors for working productively with people, school counselors are well positioned to lead this work.

References

American Evaluation Association. (2011). *Public statement on cultural competence in evaluation.* Fairhaven, MA.

American School Counselor Association. (2012). *The ASCA National Model: A framework for school counseling programs* (3rd ed.). Alexandria, VA.

Cronbach, L. J. (1982). *Designing evaluations of educational and social programs.* San Francisco, CA: Jossey-Bass.

Donaldson, S. I. (2007). *Program theory-driven evaluation science: Strategies and applications.* New York, NY: Psychology Press Taylor & Francis Group.

Fitzpatrick, J. L., Sanders, J. R., & Worthen, B. R. (2011). *Program evaluation: Alternative approaches and practical guidelines* (4th ed.). Upper Saddle River, NJ: Pearson Education, Inc.

Preskill, H. & Jones, N. (2009). *A practical guide for engaging stakeholders in developing evaluation questions.* Robert Wood Johnson Foundation Evaluation Series.

Trevisan, M. S. & Carey, J. C. (2020). Evaluating intercultural programs and interventions. In A. Portera, R. Moodley, & M. Milani (Eds.), *Intercultural mediation, counselling and psychotherapy in Europe.* Cambridge Scholars, UK.

Yarbrough, D. B., Shulha, L. M., Hopson, R. K., & Caruthers, F. A. (2010). *The Program Evaluation Standards: A guide for evaluators and evaluation users* (3rd ed.). Thousand Oaks, CA: Corwin Press.

6 The Evaluation Design and Methods

Questions to Consider

- What is the relationship between evaluation questions and evaluation designs?
- What are quantitative designs and when are they most appropriate?
- What are the most common quantitative evaluation designs?
- How are quantitative data typically analyzed?
- What are qualitative designs and when are they most appropriate?
- What are some useful ways to analyze data in qualitative evaluations?
- What are mixed-methods designs and when are they most appropriate?
- What are the JCSEE Program Evaluation Standards for quality evaluation designs?

Vignette

Kael developed a support group for high school students whose parents were divorcing. **Based on the logic model he created,** he wanted to know, **"Does the group improve the well-being and academic behavior of participating students?"** Since this was the first time the group was implemented, he also wanted to know, **"How can the group be improved?"** He asked participating students to complete a standardized mental health symptoms checklist before and after the group. *He collected data on the participating students' attendance and grades before and after participation.* In addition, **he developed a structured interview that addressed participants' experiences in the group and solicited the opinions of 10 former participants about how the group could be improved. He analyzed the quantitative data with a dependent t-test and used thematic content analysis to analyze the qualitative data. He found that after the group, students reported less anxiety and depression and had higher rates of attendance. The participating group members strongly suggested that they found the structured group activities to be most helpful and recommended spending much less time on open group discussions. Kael used the evaluation information to advocate for continuing the group with the suggested modifications to improve its effectiveness.**

Design and Methods for School Counseling Evaluation

After you have used your logic model to develop your evaluation questions, it is time to select your evaluation design and the associated measures and procedures that you will use to answer your questions. In general, you have three choices for designs: quantitative designs, qualitative designs, and mixed-methods designs (which involve both qualitative and quantitative approaches). This chapter and the subsequent two chapters, address the fundamental considerations in choosing an evaluation design, collecting data, and analyzing data. These chapters are not intended to provide a comprehensive foundation in research design; teach how to develop surveys and interviews; or teach how to analyze qualitative or quantitative data. These chapters are intended to complement training and coursework in these areas by illustrating how these skills are best applied in a school counseling program evaluation setting.

Quantitative designs are most useful in instances when the evaluation questions concern variables that can easily be measured with standardized educational and psychological measures or school counselor-constructed surveys. Such questions include

- Are there students with needs that the school counseling program is not reaching?
- Are the short-term outcomes being achieved?
- Are the long-term or ultimate outcomes of concern being achieved?

As is evident from the examples above, quantitative designs are most frequently associated with the summative evaluation questions where quantitative measures of outcomes are appropriate and, with formative evaluation questions, when quantitative measures of participation and short-term outcomes are available. Such questions typically address whether or not the expected outcomes of the program are being achieved but do not yield information on ways that improvements can be made.

Qualitative designs are most useful in instances when the evaluation questions involve variables that are difficult to assess with standardized quantitative measures and instances when it is important to gather complex, nuanced data in order to answer the questions related to program operation and improvement. Typical questions calling for qualitative analyses would include

- Are the intended prevention, social emotional, and other curricula being delivered with high fidelity to the intended students?
- Does the school counseling program have any unintended negative consequences?
- Does the school counseling program work better under some conditions than others?

These examples illustrate how qualitative designs are best suited to answering complex evaluation questions that require the collection and analyses of the perceptions, observations, and opinions of stakeholders. These evaluation questions require the use of interviews and open-ended surveys in data collection. These questions are most often related to how the program is operating rather than the specific outcomes of the program and are key to identifying needed program improvements. The one exception here is that the investigation of unintended negative consequences is typically a summative evaluation task.

Mixed-method evaluation designs are called for when the evaluation questions require the collection and analysis of both quantitative and qualitative measures. Comprehensive evaluations of an entire school counseling program always require a mixed design because the range of questions associated with these evaluations calls for the collection and analysis of both quantitative and qualitative data. In these evaluations, for example, it is important to know both if participation in counseling program activities is associated with measurable improvements in school behavior (e.g., attendance or disciplinary referrals) and if critical stakeholders have any useful suggestions for how the program should be improved.

BOX 6.1

Quantitative, qualitative, and mixed-methods evaluation designs have particular advantages related to specific evaluation questions.

The Evaluation Plan

Before proceeding with the actual evaluation, it is essential to have a good evaluation plan (see Table 6.1 for sample evaluation plan for True Goals). In order to develop the plan, it is necessary to determine what data will be collected, how the data will be collected, and how the data will be analyzed to answer each of the evaluation questions. This essentially involves the explicit identification of the evidence that will be examined in order to answer each evaluation question. An evaluation question concerning whether or not students' participation in a classroom-based activity delivered by school counselors led to increased engagement might be answered by collecting teachers' ratings of students' engagement before and after the activities, and determining whether or not there was a significant pre-post improvement. A question concerning identifying needed improvements of the lessons included in these classroom-based activities might be answered by identifying the themes that emerge for the phenomenological analysis of interviews with a sample of the participating students.

Designs for Analysis of Quantitative Data

The analyses of quantitative data always involve some comparison and contrast, and multiple possibilities exist. For example, the True Goals knowledge scores

Table 6.1 Sample evaluation plan for a formative evaluation of **True Goals** (**TG**)

Evaluation question	Evaluation design	Data to be collected	How data will be collected	How data will be analyzed
Is *TG* being delivered with high fidelity to the intended students?	Quantitative	Student attendance Checklist of Elements of *TG* lessons.	Counselors will take attendance at each lesson and complete Lesson Element Checklist afterward.	Summary of percentages of students attending lesson and percentages of lessons delivered.
Are the *TG* Learning Objectives being achieved?	Quantitative Design: One–Group Pretest–Posttest Design	Pretest and Posttest scores on survey measuring knowledge of concepts taught in *TG*.	Surveys given to all students before the first lesson and again after the last lesson.	Independent t-test.
Are there any unanticipated negative consequences of *TG* implementation?	Qualitative	Individual structured interviews with 3 classroom teachers.	Audiotaped individual interviews.	Thematic Content Analysis.
How can the *TG* implementation be improved?	Qualitative	Two Focus groups of counselor–implementers and students.	Audiotaped group interviews conducted 1 week after the last lesson.	Thematic Content Analysis.

of students who participated in a given intervention could be contrasted with the scores of students who did not participate. A difference between the participant group and comparison group that favors the participant group would be considered as evidence for the effectiveness of the intervention. Similarly, the pre- and post-intervention scores of participating students might be contrasted. Improvements in these scores would be considered as evidence for the effectiveness of the intervention. Both of these strategies would be considered as "weak" research designs because they do not control extraneous variables that limit the definitive conclusion that the intervention and only the intervention led to the observed improvements (see Campbell & Stanley, 1963). However, both research designs represent perfectly acceptable evaluation designs because they generate useful information that aids local decision-making. In naturalistic settings like schools, it is rarely possible to exert the level of control that is necessary to meet the rigorous evidentiary standards for experimental research. It is important to note, however, that very useful evaluation information can be obtained without the use of the most rigorous research designs.

The strength or weakness of a quantitative evaluation design refers to the degree to which it ensures that any observed significant differences can be attributed to the program or intervention rather than to other causes. The strongest designs are called "experimental" designs. The randomized control trial is an example of such a design. Experimental designs always involve the random assignment of students to "treatment" (the intervention) and "control" (students who do not receive the intervention) groups which ensures that the two groups were identical before the intervention. The strongest experimental designs are also "double blind" (during data collection neither the students nor the evaluators know which students are in the treatment or control groups) and include an "active control group" (students in the control receive a placebo intervention rather than no intervention at all) to control for the known impact of participant and evaluator expectations on the results (Campbell & Stanley, 1963).

Because of the lack of compatibility between the requirements of experimental designs and the school environment, experimental designs are infrequently used in the evaluation of school-based programs and interventions. School-based quantitative evaluations most frequently employ what are termed quasi-experimental or pre-experimental designs. Quasi-experimental designs approximate experimental designs without the random assignment of participants to treatment and control groups. Pre-experimental designs employ a single group and measure how that group changes between pre-treatment and post-treatment.

Table 6.2 summarizes the three most common quantitative evaluation designs. In the one-group pretest-posttest design (a pre-experimental design), the students who participate in an activity or intervention are measured before and after treatment. Post-treatment and pre-treatment scores are statistically analyzed, typically by means of a dependent t-test because scores are obtained from the same group of students. A significant improvement in scores is taken as evidence for an improvement related to participation.

able 6.2 Comparison of common quantitative evaluation designs

Quantitative Evaluation Design	The One-Group Pretest-Posttest Design	The Posttest-Only Control Group Design		The Nonequivalent Control Group Design	
		Treatment	Contrast	Treatment	Contrast
Pre-treatment data	X			X	X
Post-treatment data	X	X	X	X	X
Typical statistical analyses	Dependent t-test	Independent t-test		Independent t-test for Pre Independent t-test for Post	
Evidence for effectiveness	Significant improvement in scores pre vs. post- treatment.	Significant difference between treatment and contrast groups post- treatment (favoring treatment group).		No significant difference between the treatment and contrast groups pre-treatment AND significant difference between treatment and contrast groups post-treatment (favoring treatment group).	

In the posttest-only control group design (a quasi-experimental design), one treatment group participates in an activity or intervention while a second contrast group does not. Data is collected from both groups after the treatment. The two groups' post-treatment scores are statistically analyzed, typically by means of an independent t-test because the scores are obtained from different or independent groups of students. A significant difference in scores favoring the treatment group is taken as evidence for an improvement due to participation.

In the nonequivalent control group design (a quasi-experimental design), one treatment group participates in an activity or intervention while a second comparison group does not. Data is collected both before and after the treatment to help ensure that the two groups were equivalent before the treatment. The two groups are statistically analyzed on both their pre- and post-treatment scores, typically by means of independent t-tests. A pattern of results with nonsignificant differences between the groups pre-treatment scores and a significant post-treatment difference favoring the treatment group are taken as evidence for an improvement due to participation.

Often the choice among these three designs in evaluations is dictated by pragmatic considerations such as the availability of the necessary quantitative data and the cost of collecting it. When pragmatic considerations allow, it is best to use the strongest design.

Of these three, the nonequivalent control group design is the strongest, while the one-group pretest-posttest design is the weakest.

BOX 6.2

In selecting a quantitative evaluation design, it is important to consider both strength and feasibility.

Designs for Analysis of Qualitative Data

As is the case with quantitative designs, there are a number of qualitative designs that are useful in evaluation. Qualitative designs can be grouped into four major categories related to the purposes of the evaluation, the role of the evaluator, and the type of data that is collected and methods for the analysis of these data (Astalin, 2013). These four categories of designs include (1) case study, (2) grounded theory, (3) ethnography, and (4) phenomenology. With each of these categories, methods for the collection and analysis of qualitative data are available.

Case study designs involve the in-depth, holistic investigation of single individuals, programs, or policies in order to describe or explain them (Thomas, 2011). Grounded theory designs involve the systematic generation of a theory concerning a given phenomenon based upon the analysis of qualitative data that are collected and analyzed in a standardized manner (Strauss & Corbin, 1990). Ethnographic designs involve the qualitative investigation of human interactions within a defined setting and are particularly useful in identifying unspoken rules that govern these interactions (Fetterman, 1998). Finally, phenomenological designs involve describing and explaining something (e.g., a particular institution, program, or activity) through the systematic collection and analysis of the beliefs, impressions, and judgments of people who have had experience with it (Wertz, 2005). While all of these designs have a rightful place in the pantheon of evaluation methods, phenomenological designs offer practical, powerful, and easy-to-learn designs for the formative and summative evaluation of the school counseling program. Consequently, we will focus on phenomenological methods of data collection and analysis in this book. After mastering this design, you may eventually want to branch out and study the other designs to expand your evaluation toolbox.

The phenomenological analysis of qualitative data always involves the extraction of meaning from the relatively complex statements of multiple respondents. These responses may be collected in a wide variety of ways (e.g., open-ended survey questions, individual interviews, group interviews, and observation). School counselors need to be skilled in these methods.

As with quantitative analysis, multiple possibilities and approaches for qualitative phenomenological analysis exist (Patton, 2015; Rallis and Rossman, 2017), and it is important to know how the data will be analyzed before data collection begins. Using an established qualitative analysis approach is an essential aspect of assuring the trustworthiness of findings. As described in Chapter 8, thematic content analysis (Braun & Clarke, 2006) and interpretive phenomenological analysis (Smith, Flowers, & Larkin, 2009) are powerful, flexible, and appropriate ways to analyze qualitative data related to school counseling program evaluation questions. Also described in Chapter 8, strong qualitative evaluations also employ multiple strategies to ensure the trustworthiness of the findings.

BOX 6.3

With qualitative evaluation design, it is important to know how the data will be analyzed before date collection begins.

Designs for Mixed Methods

Mixed-methods evaluation designs may simply involve the use of quantitative methods to address some evaluation questions and qualitative methods to address other questions. However, in some instances, quantitative and qualitative methods are used to address the same question in two different stages, using both methods to their best advantage. The explanatory sequential mixed-methods design (Subedi, 2016) is such a powerful and flexible approach. In this design, an evaluation question is first addressed with quantitative methods typically using a larger sample and more standardized measures. This method is used to get a general understanding of underlying issues related to the evaluation questions and how different groups of respondents differ in their perspectives. Then a more focused qualitative investigation is conducted to clarify the issues identified by the initial quantitative investigation.

For example, a counselor interested in knowing how the school counseling program can be improved might administer a closed-ended item survey to program stakeholders and analyze the data separately for the different groups. If the counselor notices that different groups of parents have different levels of satisfaction with current services and/or different perceptions about additional needed services, they may use focus groups to better understand the experiences, perceptions, and needs of the identified groups. In this instance, the quantitative stage of the evaluation provides a general, overall answer to the evaluation question and indicates where greater clarity is needed. The qualitative stage zeroes in on these targeted issues and adds greater detail, nuance, and precision to answer the evaluation question. The results of the quantitative and qualitative stages are integrated to provide a full, rich answer to the evaluation question.

BOX 6.4

The explanatory sequential mixed-methods design is an especially powerful and flexible approach to evaluation.

Table 6.3 Selected JCSEE program evaluation standards that support evaluation design and methods

A6 Sound Design and Analyses	Evaluations should employ technically adequate designs and analyses that are appropriate for the evaluation purposes.
A7 Explicit Evaluation Reasoning	Evaluation reasoning leading from information and analyses to findings, interpretations, conclusions, and judgments should be clearly and completely documented.
A8 Communication and Reporting	Evaluation communications should have adequate scope and guard against misconceptions, biases, distortions, and errors.

Source: From Yarbrough, D. B. et al. (2010). *The Program Evaluation Standards: A guide for evaluators and evaluation users* (3rd ed.). Thousand Oaks, CA: Corwin Press. Reproduced with permission from the Joint Committee for Standards in Educational Evaluation.

Evaluation Standards that Support Evaluation Design and Methods

Evaluation designs are addressed in the JCSEE Program Evaluation Standards (Yarbrough et al., 2010) in the accuracy standards. The accuracy standards are intended to ensure that the results of evaluations will be truthful and dependable and that the findings and decisions are based on high-quality information. Table 6.3 provides a sample of JCSEE Program Evaluation Standards that support evaluation design and methods.

These selected JCSEE Program Evaluation Standards indicate that the evaluator needs to incorporate a relevant evaluation design so that (1) the data analysis procedures yield trustworthy findings that result in sound judgments and decisions and (2) the reasoning linking analyses to decisions is clearly explicated to eliminate the possibility of misunderstanding and distortion.

Culturally Responsive Evaluation

With both quantitative and qualitative methods, care needs to be taken to ensure that the evaluation is culturally responsive. Methodological considerations related to cultural responsiveness are reviewed in the next two chapters on quantitative and qualitative methods.

Summary

Evaluation questions can be answered by quantitative, qualitative, and/or mixed-methods evaluation designs. An evaluation plan indicates what data will be collected and how the data will be analyzed to answer each evaluation question. While an experimental design with random assignment and double-blind data collection is the ideal design, its rigorous requirements cannot typically be accommodated in naturalistic school settings. One-group pretest-posttest designs, posttest-only control group designs, and nonequivalent control group designs are useful quantitative designs for evaluating the impact of school counseling programs. Statistical comparisons are made, typically with independent and dependent t-tests. Qualitative designs include case study, grounded theory, ethnography, and phenomenology. Thematic content analysis and interpretive phenomenological analysis are useful ways to analyze qualitative data for evaluating school counseling programs. These will be discussed in Chapter 8. Mixed-methods evaluation designs employ both quantitative and qualitative strategies to answer evaluation questions. The explanatory sequential mixed-methods design is a particularly useful and efficient way to obtain rich answers to complex evaluation questions. The JCSEE Program Evaluation Standards (Yarbrough et al., 2010) identify the necessity of using and documenting good evaluation designs.

References

Astalin, P. K. (2013). Qualitative research designs: A conceptual framework. *International Journal of Social Science & Interdisciplinary Research*, 2, 118–124.

Braun, V. & Clarke, V. (2006). Using thematic analysis in psychology. *Qualitative Research in Psychology*, 3, 77–101.

Campbell, D. T. & Stanley, J. (1963). *Experimental and quasi-experimental designs for research*. Chicago, IL: Rand-McNally.

Fetterman, D. M. (1998). Ethnography. In L. Bickman, & D. J. Rog (Eds.), *Handbook of applied social research methods* (pp. 473–504). Thousand Oaks, CA: Sage Publications, Inc.

Patton, M. Q. (2015). *Qualitative research and evaluation methods* (4th ed.). Thousand Oaks, CA: Sage.

Rallis, S. F. & Rossman, G. B. (2017). *An introduction to qualitative research* (4th ed.). Thousand Oaks, CA: Sage.

Smith, J. A., Flowers, P., & Larkin, M. (2009). *Interpretative phenomenological analysis: Theory, method and research*. London: Sage.

Strauss, A. & Corbin, J. (1990). *Basics of qualitative research: Grounded theory procedures and techniques*. London: Sage.

Subedi, D. (2016). Explanatory sequential mixed method design as the third research community of knowledge claim. *American Journal of Educational Research*. 4, 570–577.

Thomas, G. (2011). A typology for the case study in social science following a review of definition, discourse, and structure. *Qualitative Inquiry*, 17(6), 511–521.

Wertz, F.J. (2005). Phenomenological research methods for counseling psychology. *Journal of Counseling Psychology*, 52, 167–177.

Yarbrough, D. B., Shulha, L. M., Hopson, R. K., & Caruthers, F. A. (2010). *The Program Evaluation Standards: A guide for evaluators and evaluation users* (3rd ed.). Thousand Oaks, CA: Corwin Press.

7 Data Analysis for Quantitative Data

Questions to Consider

- What does the ASCA National Model suggest regarding the collection and use of quantitative data in evaluation?
- What are the different types of quantitative data?
- How are quantitative data used to measure outputs, proximal outcomes, and distal outcomes of logic model activities?
- How are quantitative data used in the evaluation of the school counseling program?
- How are quantitative data analyzed?
- What are the advantages of using statistical analyses?
- What are alpha and beta errors and what can be done about them?
- What are the major considerations for using quantitative data in culturally responsive evaluations?

Vignette

Margarita conducted an annual evaluation of her school counseling program. She used the *school counseling program assessment* to determine the level of implementation of the elements of the ASCA National Model. She also conducted a *program goal analysis* to determine the extent to which the program's annual goals were addressed. **In addition, Margarita assessed students', parents', and teachers' levels of satisfaction with services using a survey that she had adapted the previous year with the input of the various stakeholder groups. She disaggregated the data according to important subgroups (e.g., parent ethnicity) and used t-tests to determine if the observed differences among the groups were statistically significant. She also used t-tests to determine if differences noted among the current levels of satisfaction and the previous year's levels of satisfaction had changed. She consulted representative stakeholder groups to help her understand her results.** Margarita used the combined program assessment, goals assessment, and stakeholders' satisfaction assessments to revise goals and identify new initiatives. She presented these changes to the principal, parents, and the school community.

The Use of Quantitative Evaluation Data in the ASCA National Model

Quantitative evaluation involves the use of numbers to describe the nature and impact of programs. The ASCA National Model (ASCA, 2012) advocates strongly for the use of quantitative evaluation data in evaluating the school counseling program and its activities. (See Chapter 2, Table 2.1, for a summary of the quantitative evaluation data included in the ASCA National Model.) The ASCA National Model indicates that counselors should monitor quantitative indicators of student and school performance that are maintained in a school data profile. This profile includes up-to-date achievement data (e.g., graduation rates and grade point averages) and behavioral data (e.g., discipline referral counts and attendance rates). Furthermore, the ASCA National Model suggests that quantitative data need to be disaggregated according to the major student subgroups in the school so that disparities in performance can be seen and addressed and activities can be evaluated to determine their ability to advance equity.

For the evaluation of specific activities, services or interventions, the ASCA National Model makes distinctions among what it calls "process data," "perception data," and "results data." Process data (e.g., number of intervention sessions and number of participants) provide a numerical description of an activity or intervention. Perception data reflect student reports of changes that students believe they have made resultant from the activity or intervention. Often, students provide a rating for various statements about their knowledge or attitude, for example, on a school counselor-developed survey or questionnaire. Results data (e.g., attendance rates and graduation rates) reflect the outcomes of the activity or intervention as reflected by existing school data contained in the school data profile. Analysis of these perceptions and results data is accomplished through the inspection of changes over time rather than through the use of more formal statistical analyses.

For the evaluation of the whole school counseling program, the ASCA National Model advocates for using a structured checklist to systematically review the components of the program and determine if all the elements identified in the ASCA National Model are present in the program. This school counseling program assessment determines, for example, if (1) a mission statement is evident, (2) calendars are being used to schedule weekly and annual program activities, (3) adequate percentages of counselor time are being spent on the delivery of direct and indirect services, and (4) results reports are being analyzed and shared with stakeholders. This assessment can be thought of as a check to determine if the ASCA National Model is being implemented onsite with fidelity. In addition, the ASCA National Model calls for an annual program goal analysis that involves the review of the quantitative results of activities and interventions contained in the reports to determine if program goals are being met. The annual program goal analysis would also identify the implications of the quantitative review for future program goals and activities of the school counseling program. According to the ASCA National Model, counselors use the results of the school counseling program assessment and the program's goal analysis to assess the strengths and weaknesses of the program, plan for program improvement, and share this information in the form of a report to the stakeholders.

As is evident, the ASCA National Model is heavily weighted toward the use of quantitative data. As noted previously, it is also heavily weighted toward conducting summative (vs. formative) evaluations of activities and interventions, using existing school data that reflect distal outcomes (vs. the collection of new data that reflect proximal outcomes), and analyzing data by inspection rather than with the support of statistical methods and tests. In addition, as noted previously, the ASCA National Model underemphasizes the extent to which stakeholders need to be involved at all stages in program evaluation including the design of the evaluation, the implementation of the evaluation, the interpretation of results, and the decisions made regarding program redesign and modification. As we discuss below, quantitative evaluation methods (and qualitative evaluation methods in the subsequent chapter) will supplement the evaluation processes included in the ASCA National Model in order to expand the capacity of school counselors to use evaluation to improve practice.

Quantitative Data and Its Different Levels

Quantitative data in evaluations are numbers that reflect the nature of a program and its impact. The primary advantages of using quantitative data are that it is relatively easy to make understandable summaries and comparisons and statistical procedures can be used to estimate how likely it is that observed differences are real and important. Examples of quantitative data include

- 50% of the parents of White students, 65% of the parents of Hispanic students, and 75% of African American students indicated that it was very important for the school counseling program to improve student engagement.
- 100 students participated in the new Possible Selves group.
- The Possible Selves group consisted of 10, 2-hour sessions.
- 40% of the students participating in the Possible Selves group were African American.
- 85% of the students who participated in the Possible Selves group indicated that all students in the school should participate in the group.
- The average post-test self-rating of participating students on a standardized measure of school engagement increased 3 points in comparison to their pre-test scores.

- The average post-test self-rating of participating students on a standardized measure of school engagement was 3 points higher than the average post-test self-rating of nonparticipating students.
- Students participating in the Possible Selves group had an average of 2 fewer absentee days in comparison to nonparticipating students in the 6 months after the Possible Selves group.

While these data are quantitative, important differences exist that determine the appropriate ways that the data can be summarized and communicated. These differences result from what is referred to as the level of measurement (Stevens, 1946) of the data. Quantitative data can represent a numerical name (nominal data), a count (ordinal data), or a scale (interval or ratio data). Nominal data are best summarized and communicated by reporting the mode or percentages. For example, we might report that most parents (70% of those who responded to a satisfaction survey) indicated that they were satisfied with program services. Ordinal data are best summarized by reporting the median (the middle score in a rank order) and/or by ranking-related statistics (e.g., quartiles). For example, we might report that students in our high school predominantly apply to colleges that are in the bottom quartile (colleges ranked in the bottom 25% of all colleges) in national rankings. Interval and ratio data are best summarized and communicated by means (averages) and related standardized statistical descriptions of variability (e.g., standard deviations). For example, we might report that senior students at our school had an average score of 55.5 on a depression screening survey, which was 0.85 standard deviation units above the national mean.

When is Quantitative Data Useful?

Quantitative data is useful in both formative and summative evaluations. Quantitative evaluation data can be collected from existing student data in the school's information system, as with the ASCA National Model's (ASCA, 2012) school data profile. However, these data are more useful in measuring distal outcomes in summative evaluation of program activities and in the summative evaluation of the program as a whole.

To measure the outputs and proximal outcomes of activities and interventions, it is typically necessary to collect additional information in the form of self-made or standardized surveys. These surveys are used to determine whether or not the specific activity resulted in the changes that are expected to occur immediately after the activity. These changes can be in students' knowledge, attitudes, and/or behavior. Confirming that these expected changes occur is an important part of a formative evaluation and an important first step in a summative evaluation.

It is nearly always preferable to use a standardized survey as compared with a self-made survey with unknown psychometric properties. However, while some "manualized" curricula have standardized instruments to measure outputs, most often the counselor-evaluator needs to create these instruments themselves.

In contrast, standardized surveys that measure proximal outcomes can almost always be found. Here the major issues are where to find these surveys and what criteria to use in selecting a survey. Proximal outcomes correspond to the short-term, measurable changes in students' school behavior and related attitudes that are expected to be evident in the weeks following participation in an activity. Surveys measuring these proximal outcomes can be completed by the students themselves or by individuals (e.g., teachers or parents) who are in a good position to observe changes in the students' behavior and demeanor.

Gathering quantitative data is also very useful in the evaluation of the school counseling program as a whole, especially when an efficient way to gather data from a large number of people is needed. The best example of this situation is the use of stakeholder satisfaction surveys to determine how satisfied the members of different stakeholder groups are with the program's current services and what new services are desired. While it is possible to find existing stakeholder instruments (see Gallant & Zhao, 2011; Rief & Enestvedt, 1993), it is most often necessary to revise these instruments to take into account local circumstances. Representatives of the different stakeholder groups ought to be involved in selecting and revising satisfaction surveys and in interpreting the results. In addition, demographic items that facilitate the disaggregation of the survey results by stakeholder groups must be part of the survey.

High-quality quantitative evaluation is dependent on the school counselor having skill in selecting and creating good instruments. Having good data that accurately reflect the knowledge, attitudes, and behaviors we wish to know about is an essential requirement for a good evaluation. Dimmitt, Carey, and Hatch (2007) provide very useful guidance on (1) how to find and select standardized surveys for use in the evaluation of the school counseling program and (2) how to develop surveys when it is necessary to do so.

BOX 7.1

Quantitative evaluation designs are called for when good measures of important variables are available or can be easily created.

Sampling Issues

Decisions need to be made regarding how much quantitative data will be collected and from whom. Given that many forms of quantitative data are relatively easy to collect (e.g., parent surveys), it is tempting to collect more data than is actually needed. From a purely statistical standpoint, more data are always better. However, from a practical standpoint, too much data can result in needless work and bog down the evaluation process. In such instances, randomly selecting participants from the larger group makes sense. Random selection helps ensure that the data are unbiased and representative of the larger group. Often it is helpful to sample by random selection within defined demographic categories, as described below.

There are instances when data should be collected from all participants. For example, if 20 5th-grade students are participating in a group receiving an intervention that is being evaluated, it makes good sense to collect data from all 20. If a comparison to a contrast group that is not receiving the intervention is to be made, however, it makes sense to create this group by sampling from the participants' peers rather than gathering data from all the other nonparticipating 5th graders. Two sampling strategies could be considered: (1) creating a contrast group by randomly selecting 20 nonparticipating 5th graders or (2) creating a contrast group by selecting 20 nonparticipating 5th graders who are matched on important characteristics (e.g., gender, racial/ethnic group, and grades). In general, matched sampling results in more sensitive analyses. Because the intervention and contrast groups are highly similar, it is easier to detect a difference due to treatment.

In instances in which large numbers of respondents could contribute data (e.g., parental questionnaires), it is advisable to sample rather than collect data from everyone.

Table 7.1 contains a summary of different approaches. In making the decision about sampling, it is important to first consider how the data will need to

Table 7.1 Three strategies for collecting parent satisfaction survey data

Strategy	Advantages	Disadvantages
Collect data from all parents	Everyone has the opportunity to voice his or her opinion.	Can result in too much data, making data collection, data entry, and data analyses costly and difficult.
Collect data from a random sample of parents	The amount of data to be collected can be set at a manageable level for efficient data collection, entry, and analysis.	Proportionate representation of important subgroups may not occur due to randomness. Analyses and understanding of important subgroup differences may not be possible due to low numbers. Parents not included in the sample may be concerned that their opinions may not be desired or respected.
Collect data from a stratified random sample of parents	The amount of data to be collected can be set at a manageable level for efficient data collection, entry, and analysis. Adequate representation of parents from important subgroups can be ensured.	Parents not included in the sample may be concerned that their opinions may not be desired or respected.

be disaggregated for analyses and interpretations. For example, if the major parental subgroups in a school are African Americans, Latinos/as, and Whites, it would be important to sample so that all the subgroups will end up contributing enough data to support valid analyses and interpretations. Randomly selecting 50 parents from each group would be an appropriate approach in this case. You might also consider creating a stratified random sample if it is important to understand perceptions of parents as a whole in addition to each subgroup's perceptions. With stratified random sampling, the sample is selected so that there is proportional representation of all of the important subgroups. Here, a target number (e.g., 50) would be set for the smallest subgroup, and target numbers would be set for the other groups that are proportional to each group's representation in the school population. For example, in an elementary school that has 20% African American families, 30% Latino/a families, and 50% White families, the target would be to obtain parental surveys from 50 African American parents, 75 Latino/a parents, and 125 White parents.

Finally, when making decisions about numbers to sample, it is important to consider how much data may be lost during the data collection process. It is always helpful to set sampling targets a bit high to take into account data loss. It is also important to conduct data collection in a way that minimizes loss and maximizes return rates.

Common Ways to Analyze Quantitative Data

Quantitative data need to be analyzed to determine their meaning so that sound decisions can be made. The ASCA National Model (ASCA, 2012) advocates for the use of simple forms of analysis (e.g., comparing group differences by observation). This process, though logical, lacks other forms of analyses that could provide more confidence with respect to the magnitude of the differences observed and therefore the inferences drawn about the program. Use of statistical tests to augment the observations provides powerful and important additional information to improve the accuracy of the findings and help improve program decisions.

Inspection and Graphic Analysis

Inspection and graphic analysis are simple approaches to quantitative data analysis. Here, corresponding data elements are visually inspected for apparently obvious differences. This is done either by just looking at the differences or by graphing the differences to make inspection easier. For example, a high school counselor evaluating an intervention designed to enhance students' engagement might gather quantitative data on students' attendance. The school counselor found that after the intervention, only 5% of the students who participated had 5 or more days absent during the following term, while 15% of students who did not participate had 5 or more days absent in the same period. Inspection suggests that there is a large difference between the two groups, but unless this difference is real—that is, if the same intervention is repeated with another group of students, a similar difference would be found between participating and nonparticipating students—decisions based on it are tentative or even uncertain. Inspection cannot adequately account for the amount of natural variability in the data and hence cannot discern the amount of confidence that should be placed in a given conclusion.

Relatedly, two corresponding pieces of quantitative data can look similar but actually be different in important ways. For example, a high school stakeholder survey might reveal that 5% of the parents of White students and 9% of the parents of Hispanic students believe that bullying needs to be addressed better by the school counseling program. While these two values look quite similar, appearances can be deceiving. If these data were based on 20 White parents and 200 Hispanic parents, they suggest that only 1 White family saw the need for additional bullying prevention work while 18 Hispanic families saw this need.

Statistical Analysis

Statistical analysis provides additional support for decision-making by enhancing the accuracy of findings and conclusions. Statistical analyses take the amount of variability in the data and the amount of data into account to improve decision-making. Different types of statistical procedures are needed for different types of data. Different types of statistical procedures are also needed for comparisons of independent groups (e.g., separate treatment vs. comparison groups) versus for comparisons of the same group with itself at different times (e.g., pre-treatment vs. post-treatment).

There are a dizzying number of statistical procedures (both simple and complex) that can be used by school counselors. We recommend that all school counselors need to be able to conduct a small subset of these analyses and be knowledgeable enough about what is possible with statistical analyses in order to be able to consult with a statistician when more complex procedures would be appropriate and useful.

We suggest that all school counselors should be able to conduct

- Chi-square tests of the differences between independent treatment and comparison groups.
- Chi-square tests of the differences in the same group over time (e.g., between pre-treatment and post-treatment).
- Independent t-tests of the differences between independent treatment and comparison groups.
- Dependent t-tests of the differences in the same group over time (e.g., between pre-treatment and post-treatment).

These four analytic procedures will allow school counselors to contrast data from two independent groups and from one group over time to determine how much confidence should be placed in the conclusion that the apparent differences between the groups are real, or said another way, not due to random fluctuation in the data.

BOX 7.2

Using statistical tests to analyze quantitative evaluation data offers several important advantages over visual inspection.

Choosing Among Statistical Tests

In choosing the right test, there are a number of important considerations. Certain tests are only useful for comparing two groups. T-tests, for example, can be used for comparing scores from two different groups or the scores from a single group at two different times. If you want to compare three or more groups, a different test is needed (e.g., F-test).

In addition, the level of measurement of the data has an impact on the selection of a test. With nominal level data (e.g., where one wants to make a comparison between the percentages of male and female students who pass a test), a t-test would be inappropriate because it makes no sense to calculate a mean of passes and failures. Here a chi-square test would be the right choice.

Finally, some tests make assumptions that are important to consider regarding the nature of the quantitative data. Statistical tests occur in two broad families: nonparametric tests and parametric tests. Nonparametric tests (e.g., chi-square and rank-order tests) make few assumptions about the raw data. Parametric tests require the estimation of some population parameters (e.g., the mean and standard deviation of the population) and typically make several assumptions that allow for the estimation of the rarity of observed group differences. The most important of these assumptions is that the data are normally distributed (normalcy assumption) and variances are equal (equal variance assumption) among the groups. T-tests, for example, assume that the scores analyzed are distributed in a bell-shaped curve and that the variability of the scores of the two groups are approximately equal.

Parametric tests have more power than nonparametric tests, so it is always better to use them if they are appropriate. There is less chance of making a beta error (see next section). Before performing a parametric test, its best to look at a frequency distribution of the raw data to make sure that it approximates a bell-shaped curve and to inspect the standard deviations of the groups to make sure they are approximately equal. If gross violations of these assumptions are noted, the use of a nonparametric test may be called for. Figure 7.1 presents a decision tree to summarize how to decide between parametric and nonparametric analyses.

Because the dependent t-test statistically analyzes the differences between pre- and post-treatment scores for a single group of students, a normal distribution is ensured (with a sufficiently large group size). However, with an independent t-test, the distribution of scores in the two groups should be checked. If the scores are

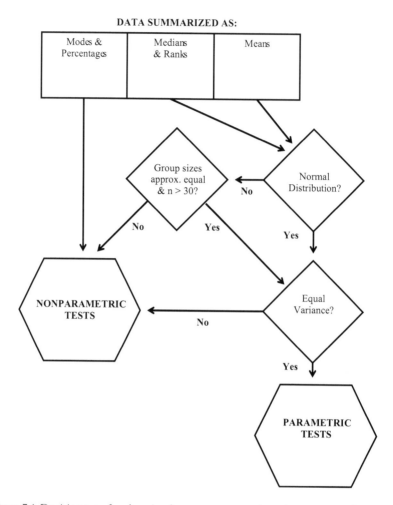

Figure 7.1 Decision tree for choosing between parametric and nonparametric tests.

not distributed normally, it is still possible to use an independent t-test if the group numbers are adequate (larger than 30) and the group sizes are approximately equal. Under these conditions, the independent t-test still yields reasonably accurate results even though the normalcy assumption has been violated.

However, neither t-test is robust regarding violations of the equal variance assumption. While complicated statistical corrections are possible, the best course of action is typically to use a nonparametric test instead.

Alpha Levels and Possible Errors

Statistical tests provide information on the probability that an observed difference in some statistic (e.g., mean, median rank, percentage) between two groups (i.e., separate treatment and comparison groups, or of the same group before and after treatment) is likely to be real and due to the intervention, rather than to be due to chance fluctuations in the sample of data. These tests take into account the size of the difference between the groups, the number of participants in the groups, and the variability of the participants' scores for the given statistic.

The alpha level, established prior to computing the statistical test, is the decision point that is used to make the claim that a difference observed is due to the intervention and not random fluctuation in the data. For research purposes, a "conservative" alpha level (.05, .01, .001) is generally used to help prevent spurious results from being widely disseminated. In evaluations, however, a less conservative alpha level is often used (.20 or .10) to help minimize the possibility that an effective activity is erroneously considered ineffective (Dimmitt, Carey, & Hatch, 2007).

Statistical tests computed with statistical software today generate an alpha statistic that reflects the actual probability of observing a particular difference between groups. After computing a t-test for a difference between two means, for example, if the alpha statistic shows a probability of the observed difference between groups at .03 with a previously established significance level of .05, then the claim is made that the difference is due to the program intervention (since .03 is less than .05). The historic phrase "statistically significant" can also be used.

An alpha level established at .05, for example, signals that the observed difference between the groups would only be expected to occur 5% of the time by chance. The school counselor is using .05 as a pre-specified decision point to signal how unlikely the difference must be in order to claim the difference is not due to chance but due to the intervention. The decision point signals the amount of certainty in the determination. In other words, we can be 95% certain that the difference between the groups is due to the program intervention. Of course, if we conclude that the difference is real, we will still be wrong 5% of the time.

There are two types of mistakes that we can make in using statistical tests to assist our decision-making. We may conclude that two groups are really different due to the program intervention when in fact they are not. This is called an alpha error. We may conclude that there is no evidence that the two groups are different due to the program intervention when in fact they are. This is called a beta error.

There are real consequences to these mistakes. Making an alpha error may mean that an ineffective intervention is continued the next year even though it does not really produce the desired benefits. Making a beta error may mean that an effective intervention is discontinued even though it produces real benefits for students. Both of these errors are potentially costly! Table 7.2 summarizes these errors.

Alpha and beta errors are related to each other. Setting the probability level to minimize alpha errors (concluding there is a difference when there is not)

Table 7.2 Consequences and probabilities of making alpha and beta errors with different alpha levels for a statistical test

		Alpha level of statistical test			
Error	Consequence	.25	.10	.05	.01
Alpha Error	Continue an ineffective program	High probability	Medium Probability	Low probability	Very low probability
Beta Error	Discontinue an effective program	Very low probability	Low probability	Medium Probability	High probability

increases the probability of making a beta error (concluding that there is no real difference when there is).

BOX 7.3

In evaluations, a less conservation alpha level is typically used to avoid inappropriate conclusions about program effectiveness.

Quantitative Approaches and Culturally Responsive Evaluation

The American Evaluation Association's (2011) *Public Statement on Cultural Competence in Evaluation* underscores the need for ensuring that design and measurement strategies are appropriate for the cultural contexts of particular evaluation settings. Using quantitative evaluation strategies presents some unique challenges.

Frierson, Hood, and Hughes (2010) have indicated that care needs to be taken in the selection and/or development of quantitative surveys and instruments. They note that whenever possible, evaluation forms and instruments should be selected that have been used previously in similar cultural settings with success. They suggest that using standardized instruments that have been normed with diverse populations helps ensure the validity of the findings. When these types of instruments are not available, they suggest modifying the instrument to ensure cultural appropriateness.

In developing surveys, it is important to consider linguistic diversity by creating equivalent surveys in multiple languages and checking that the surveys are easily readable (Public Policy Associates, 2015). It is highly advisable to have a group of stakeholders review the instruments beforehand to evaluate their utility and appropriateness (Centers for Disease Control and Prevention, 2010).

Frierson, Hood, and Hughes (2010) also advocate for disaggregating quantitative data whenever possible during analyses to make sure that any findings that are unique to a given subgroup will not be inadvertently lost. For example, a parent satisfaction survey should be designed so that the data from important subgroups of parents (e.g., racial/ethnic groups, socioeconomic status groups) can be analyzed separately so that the perceptions of all parents can be taken into account. As an additional example, the outcomes of a prevention program should be analyzed separately for students from different subgroups to determine if everyone benefits equally.

Summary

The use of quantitative data in evaluations has some distinct advantages. Being able to measure important characteristics of the program and important program outcomes using numbers makes comparisons easier and enables the use of statistical analyses procedures that can improve decision-making. Some numerical measures are included in existing school data. However, school counselors need to be able to develop sound measures for important variables that are not available in typical school data. This is especially true for formative and summative evaluations that need to measure outputs and proximal outcomes. It is often useful to sample data rather than collecting it from all potential participants. Here, care must be taken so that enough representative data are collected for analyses. Statistical analyses offer some special advantages over visual and graphic inspection, including information on the likelihood that the observed group differences occurred by chance. In evaluation, a less conservative alpha level (.10 or .20) is often used in statistical analyses to help prevent beta errors, inaccurately concluding that an intervention had no impact when in fact it had. Finally, ensuring the validity of an evaluation through the use of culturally responsive practices is essential. Ensuring the appropriateness of the quantitative data collection instruments and the disaggregation of data during analyses are particularly important.

References

American Evaluation Association. (2011). *Public statement on cultural competence in evaluation.* Fairhaven, MA: Author.

American School Counselor Association. (2012). *The ASCA national model: A framework for school counseling programs* (3rd ed.). Alexandria, VA: Author.

Centers for Disease Control and Prevention. (2010). *Practical strategies for culturally competent evaluation.* Atlanta, GA: US Department of Health and Human Services.

Dimmitt, C., Carey J. C., & Hatch, T. (2007). *Evidence-based school counseling: Making a difference with data-driven practices.* New York, NY: Corwin Press.

Frierson, H. T., Hood, S., & Hughes, G. B. (2010) A guide to conducting culturally responsive evaluations. In J. Frechtling (Ed.), *The 2010 user-friendly handbook for project evaluation* (pp. 75–93). Washington, DC: National Science Foundation.

Gallant D. J. & Zhao, J. (2011). High school students' perceptions of school counseling services. *Counseling Outcome Research and Evaluation, 2,* 87–100.

Public Policy Associates. (2015). *Considerations for conducting evaluation using a culturally responsive/racial equity lens.* Lansing, MI: Author.

Rief, J. M. & Enestvedt, J. K. (1993). *The Minnesota school counselors' model of developmental guidance and counseling.* Minneapolis, MN: Minnesota School Counselors' Association.

Stevens, S. S. (1946). On the theory of scales of measurement. *Science, 103*, 677–680.

8 Data Analysis for Qualitative Data

Questions to Consider

- How can qualitative data be collected and used in the evaluation of ASCA National Model programs?
- What are the methods for collecting qualitative evaluation data?
- What are the methods for analyzing qualitative data in evaluations?
- What are the strategies for ensuring the trustworthiness of qualitative evaluations?
- What are the major considerations for using qualitative data in culturally responsive evaluations?

Vignette

Ellen, a counselor working in a middle school, *implemented and evaluated a classroom-based anti-bullying curriculum*. In addition to using the closed-ended student surveys provided by the curriculum developer, Ellen decided to **interview the 4th- and 5th-grade teachers to ask, "Are there any unanticipated negative consequences associated with the implementation of the curriculum?" She developed a short, structured interview guide, interviewed each of the teachers, and analyzed the recorded data using thematic content analysis.** A major theme that emerged was that the teachers felt reluctant to address bullying issues themselves when she was not present because they were unsure of what to do and did not want to be inconsistent with what she was teaching the students. In response, Ellen circulated readings on the anti-bullying curriculum to the teachers, organized a short orientation to the curriculum for them, and asked them to stay in the classroom and observe her while she was teaching the anti-bullying lessons. Subsequent evaluations indicated that these changes enhanced student learning, attitude change, and behavior change.

Qualitative Evaluation Data in the ASCA National Model

Qualitative evaluation is often insufficient to document the outcomes of a program or its associated activities and interventions. However, qualitative evaluation approaches are necessary to document the human impact of the program on participants and to identify the ways in which the program can be improved (Patton, 2015). Qualitative data reflect the subjective experiences, opinions, and judgments of the program's participants, implementers, and stakeholders and provides important insights into the operation, limitations, and ways to improve the program.

The ASCA National Model (ASCA, 2012) does not emphasize the use of qualitative data in evaluating school counseling programs and their activities. This may be because the ASCA National Model is focused on using evaluation to produce persuasive evidence of the impact of school counseling programs using quantitative data that are of particular interest to school administrators (e.g., student attendance rates, graduation rates, and disciplinary referral rates). While this is understandable, failing to use qualitative approaches to their best advantage will limit the ability of an evaluation to generate information needed to improve programs.

Qualitative evaluation requires that data be collected and analyzed in a methodical fashion. Qualitative data can be collected in a wide variety of ways (e.g., documents, observations, interviews). Qualitative data can be analyzed in a number of ways such as, by thematic content analysis (Braun & Clarke, 2006), interpretative phenomenological analysis (Smith, Flowers, & Larkin, 2009), and grounded theory analysis (Glaser & Strauss, 1967). Below we will describe the most useful and straightforward ways to collect and analyze qualitative data in the evaluation of a school counseling program. Additional useful information on qualitative evaluation methods can be found in both Patton (2015) and Rallis and Rossman (2017).

How to Collect Qualitative Data

School counselors have a particular advantage regarding qualitative data collection. School counselors know how to suspend judgment, ask open-ended questions, probe for understanding, and avoid asking leading questions that constrain and bias clients' responses. School counselors are experts at individual interviews. Within group interview settings, school counselors are skilled at creating a safe environment, drawing people out, and helping them add to and build on each other's understandings. All these skills are necessary in constructing qualitative data collection instruments and strategies and in collecting qualitative data.

Open-Ended Survey Questions

Using open-ended items in a survey is the easiest way to collect important qualitative data. Open-ended items require a written response from survey participants while closed-ended items only require the participant to select from among a set of pre-determined responses. Open-ended items can be added to a closed-ended item survey in order to create the opportunity for participants to add insights that cannot be anticipated beforehand by the school counselor. For example, at the end of a closed-ended stakeholder satisfaction survey, an item might ask, "In your opinion how could the school counselors work more effectively with parents?" Alternatively, an entire survey may be comprised of only open-ended questions. A major advantage of open-ended survey questions is that they efficiently generate a written record of a large number of responses that represent the data upon which subsequent qualitative analyses are based.

All open-ended survey items should be aligned with an evaluation question. To avoid confusion, each survey item should address only one issue. Open-ended survey items should be written in simple straightforward language, avoiding jargon, to ensure that everyone will understand the question in the same way and has sufficient experience and knowledge to formulate an informed response to the question. In addition, all items should be screened to make sure that they do not inadvertently bias participants' responses. It is advisable to invite a small group of stakeholders to pre-review these items, to observe them while they answer the questions, and to interview them in order to identify needed modifications and revisions. Table 8.1 provides a sample of open-ended survey questions, problems with each question, and a possible revision.

Structured Individual Interviews

Evaluations also use individual interviews to collect qualitative data. Typically, these interviews are recorded for subsequent analysis. This may involve careful note-taking during the interview, audio recording, and subsequent transcription. Due to the time-consuming nature of the data collection and analysis processes, it is unwise to try to collect data from a large sample. Interviews are best used for collecting in-depth data from a relatively small sample of people who are

Table 8.1 Open-ended survey questions

Original item	Problem(s)	Revised item(s)
What additional things should the school counselors do to serve parents and students better?	Two issues in the same item	What additional things should the school counselors do to serve parents better? What additional things should the school counselors do to serve students better?
What do you consider to be the primary competencies that the comprehensive developmental school counseling program should build in all students?	Overly complex language Professional jargon	What are the most important skills that students need to learn?
What problems have you personally experienced that have kept you from connecting with your child's counselor?	Bias	How would you suggest we change what we do in order to ensure that parents have better access to counselors?

intentionally selected for their ability to shed important light on the evaluation questions being examined.

Before the structured interview, an interview guide needs to be developed. The guide contains a small number (5–6) of general questions that are aligned with the evaluation question(s) and that will be presented in the same way to everyone. Potential prompts and follow-up questions are planned to encourage all interviewees to give full, thoughtful responses. The interview questions are sequenced so that the easier, less personal, questions will come first in order to help build rapport. For the sake of efficiency, school counselors need to discipline themselves to avoid letting the interview veer off on tangents (no matter how entertaining and interesting the tangents may be). The purpose of the interview is to gather the necessary information that will be used to answer the evaluation question(s) in as efficient a manner as is possible. Table 8.2 provides a sample interview guide to be used with graduating high school seniors to gather data to help answer the evaluation question, "How can college counseling services be improved?"

Focus Group Interviews

Focus groups are efficient and effective ways to collect important evaluation data. When designed and conducted properly, they present an opportunity

Table 8.2 Sample individual interview guide: Interview with graduating high school seniors to gather data to help answer the evaluation question, "How can college counseling services be improved?"

#	Question	Prompts/follow-ups
1	Can you describe your decisions about college and how you made them?	Probe for involvement of self, family, friends, and school personnel.
2	What college choice-related activities did you participate in and how helpful were they?	If not mentioned, ask about career day, interest inventory, online college information session, family meeting, financial aid/scholarship information, college application sessions.
3	What were the most helpful school activities?	Prompt for 2nd response if not given.
4	What were the least helpful school activities?	Prompt for 2nd response, if not given.
5	What are the most imports things that counselors can do in addition, or can do differently, in order to be more helpful to students as they make college decisions?	Prompt for complete response: do in addition and do differently.
6	Is there anything that I forgot to ask you that would help me understand better how the school can be of more help to students as they make their college choices?	Allow time for thought.

to collect a range of perspectives on important evaluation questions based on a focus-group discussion. According to Denscombe (2007), "a focus group consists of a small group of people, usually between six and nine in number, who are brought together by a trained moderator to explore attitudes and perceptions, feelings and ideas about a topic" (p.115).

A record is kept of the focus-group discussion and analyzed using qualitative analysis procedures.

Focus groups are best used to answer complex evaluation questions where there are likely to be multiple perspectives and where group discussion would likely be helpful in surfacing answers to the questions. For example, focus groups would be an appropriate way to address the evaluation question, "Does the school counseling program have any unintended negative consequences?"

Before a focus group is conducted, the evaluator needs to decide who will be included in the group, how many groups will be conducted, and what questions will be asked to guide the focus group discussion. There is a wide range of opinion about the optimal composition of focus groups (Krueger & Casey, 2000, Bloor et al., 2001). In general, focus groups ought to be homogeneous enough so that members can talk together freely, openly, and honestly, yet be heterogeneous enough so that a wide range of perspectives on the evaluation question is available. In school counseling program evaluations, this will typically mean that a focus group will be composed of students, counselors, teachers, parents, or administrators with the group's members selected intentionally for their ability to offer a range of perspectives. It may be necessary to convene separate groups to discuss the same questions in order to understand how different stakeholders understand the issue.

Developing a guide for the focus group involved is necessary to help keep the discussion focused on the evaluation question (Anderson, 1998; Bloor et al., 2001). Typically, the guide includes a description of the purpose of the interview, an orienting question, a series of transition questions, the key questions(s), and an ending question. Questions are always phrased in an open-ended fashion. Table 8.3 contains a sample focus group guide with a group of teachers to help address the evaluation question, "Does the school counseling program have any unintended negative consequences?"

BOX 8.1

Qualitative evaluation data can be collected in a wide variety of ways including open-ended surveys, interviews, and focus groups.

Focus groups require lots of discussion time and typically require 1–2 hours. During the interview, the evaluator introduces the purpose of the group and facilitates a group discussion. The evaluator uses group counseling skills to help members express their opinions and ideas, add to each other's perspectives, challenge each other's beliefs and conclusions, and identify points of agreement

Table 8.3 Sample focus group guide for teachers addressing the evaluation question, "Does the school counseling program have any unintended negative consequences?"

Purpose	We are here today to identify whether there are any unintended negative consequences for students, teachers, and parents that result from the way we are implementing our school counseling program.
Orienting Questions	What are the possible ways that students, parents, and teachers are not being served presently?
	What are the possible ways that students, parents, and teachers are being harmed?
Transition Questions	What instances have you seen of students being underserved by the program or even harmed by their interactions with the program?
	What instances have you seen of parents being underserved by the program or even harmed by their interactions with the program?
	What instances have you seen of teachers being underserved by the program or even harmed by their interactions with the program?
Key Question	What changes could be made in the program to minimize the unintended negative consequences for students, parents, and teachers that we have identified?
Ending Question	In answering this question today, is there anything we have forgotten to consider that will help improve the school counseling program?

and disagreement. In addition, the evaluator needs to manage the discussion to promote the inclusion of all members by encouraging open communication, drawing out quiet members, managing overly chatty members, and cutting off any comments that may make the conversation seem unsafe for any members. The complexity of this group facilitator role makes it difficult for an evaluator to also keep a record of the conversation. The focus group can be recorded or a second evaluator may participate as a note keeper.

Using Thematic Content Analysis in Evaluation

No matter how qualitative data is collected, it is necessary to reduce and analyze the raw data in order to extract information and determine its meanings. While there are a large number of ways to approach this analytic process, thematic content analysis (Braun & Clarke, 2006) and interpretative phenomenological analysis (Smith, Flowers, & Larkin, 2009) are particularly flexible and useful approaches. Thematic content analysis can be used with virtually any type of qualitative data. Interpretative phenomenological analysis is more time consuming and complex but yields detailed information on interviewees' personal understandings of phenomena related to the evaluation questions. It is best reserved for the analyses of in-depth interviews.

Thematic content analysis is one of the most straightforward ways to analyze qualitative data (Maguire & Delahunt, 2017). Braun and Clarke (2006) suggest a six-step analytic process: (1) become familiar with the data, (2) generate initial codes, (3) search for themes, (4) review themes, (5) define themes, and

(6) write-up. To start, the school counselor reads through all the raw data in order to get a general sense of what it contains and makes general notes to guide subsequent analyses. Next, the school counselor scrolls through the data identifying the sections that pertain to the evaluation question that is being examined and codes each identified section with a short phrase that summarizes its meaning. After the data is coded, the school counselor examines the codes to identify clusters of related codes or "themes." Names are given to the themes that reflect aspects of answers to the evaluation questions. These themes are then reviewed to determine if they make sense, are supported by the data, are organized appropriately, and present a comprehensive picture of the data. At this point, the existing themes may be combined or divided and new codes may be added. The school counselor then defines these refined themes and describes how the themes appear to be related to each other. The themes, definitions, and description of hypothetical relationships are then written up in a form that will appear in a evaluation report.

Using Interpretive Phenomenological Analysis in Evaluation

Smith et al. (2009) have described a similar process for analyzing qualitative data that involves five steps. First, the data from the first respondent is reviewed several times by the school counselor who takes notes on the respondent's beliefs and personal understandings. Second, the school counselor re-reviews the data and notes and writes concise themes that reflect the respondent's expressions. Third, these themes are then clustered into meaningful chunks and superordinate themes are identified. Fourth, the school counselor next creates a table of the themes which identifies the most salient and important themes. Fifth, the school counselor moves on to analyze the data from the next respondent, either starting fresh or using the existing table of themes as the starting point in the subsequent analysis. The endpoint of the process is a summary of the themes that reflect how all respondents understood and evaluated phenomena that are related to the particular evaluation question being investigated.

Ensuring the Trustworthiness of Qualitative Findings

Because of the subjective nature of qualitative approaches to evaluation, it is necessary to attend to the trustworthiness of the evaluation findings. According to Guba (1981), trustworthy findings are findings that are credible, dependable, confirmable, and transferable. Every qualitative evaluation should employ multiple strategies to ensure trustworthiness (Shenton, 2004).

Evaluations that use well-accepted methods for collecting and analyzing qualitative data are more likely to yield trustworthy findings. If the school counselor clearly identifies their own beliefs and biases at the initial stages of the evaluation, they will be in a better position to conduct an evaluation that leads to trustworthy findings. The school counselor can do this by writing a few brief paragraphs summarizing their reflections on the program and its operations. The triangulation of findings to verify their consistency across different groups (and/or across different methods) also helps ensure trustworthiness. In addition, periodic debriefing with peers during the evaluation also helps a school counselor conduct an unbiased qualitative evaluation. Finally, having interviewees and/or stakeholders review the analyses and interpretations of qualitative evaluations further ensures trustworthiness.

BOX 8.2

In qualitative evaluations, steps must be takes to ensure the trustworthiness of the data.

Qualitative Approaches and Culturally Responsive Evaluation

Qualitative evaluation approaches present some unique challenges in multicultural settings. In order to conduct a culturally responsive evaluation, special care must be taken in the collection, analysis, and interpretation of qualitative data.

Language preferences and facility present a challenge to the collection of valid information. Ideally, interviews ought to be conducted in the language of the stakeholders. The next best alternative is conducting an interview through an interpreter.

Being able to bridge differences in language, however, is only a start. Interviewees need to feel comfortable and safe in interview settings. Interviewers need to be sensitive to the societal dynamics that may be operating in the interview setting. These dynamics will affect interviewee comfort and openness. Interviewers should actively work to create a safe interview setting (Centers for Disease Control and Prevention, 2010; Public Policy Associates, 2015).

In addition, interviewee nonverbal behavior affects the conduct of interviews. Culture has a major influence on cues (e.g., eye contact, shifts in gaze, gestures, pauses) that interviewers use to gauge interest and understanding and contextualize verbal expression (Frierson, Hood, & Hughes, 2010). Due to the subliminal level in which nonverbal communication operates, misinterpretation is highly likely. Interviewers need to have sufficient experience with cross-cultural communication to be able to accurately ascertain the meaning of interviewees' nonverbal communication (Public Policy Associates, 2015).

Group interviews (e.g., focus groups) can be especially problematic and need to be planned, conducted, and interpreted in a culturally responsive manner. For example, with parent stakeholder focus groups, it is important to consider whether the groups should be composed of culturally heterogeneous or homogeneous parents. In making this decision, a school counselor should ask himself or herself

- Considering the evaluation questions and the multicultural dynamics, are members of all the parental subgroups likely to feel safe enough to contribute openly to the focus group discussion?
- Are there some potential advantages associated with having a multicultural discussion of the evaluation questions?
- Are there any anticipatable problems that may arise in a multicultural discussion of the evaluation questions?
- Do I have adequate interview skills to effectively manage these potential problems (e.g., conflict that may occur in this discussion)?

Cultural responsiveness also needs to be expressed in the analysis and interpretation of qualitative evaluation data. The meaning of a piece of qualitative data can only be accurately ascertained within the cultural context through which the data was collected. School counselors need to take care to apply analytic procedures and interpret findings with a proper consideration of respondents' cultural frame of reference. School counselors need to be able to identify when their own biases are affecting analysis and interpretation. They also need to have sufficient experience and cultural competence with members of the target group to fully comprehend the meaning and nuances of the responses (Public Policy Associates, 2015). Finally, to ensure trustworthiness, it is important to having respondents and stakeholders review the analyses and interpretations.

Summary

Using qualitative evaluation approaches in evaluating a school counseling program, its associated activities, and interventions is necessary to answer important questions related to program improvement. Qualitative approaches to evaluation align naturally with the existing skillset of school counselors. While qualitative data can be collected in many ways, open-ended survey questions, structured individual interviews, and focus group interviews are particularly well suited to evaluation of a school counseling program. Similarly, thematic content analysis and interpretative phenomenological analysis are well-accepted methods for the analysis of qualitative data and well suited for evaluation of a school counseling program. No matter which methods are employed, every qualitative evaluation should include multiple strategies to ensure the trustworthiness of its findings. In order to conduct a culturally responsive evaluation special care must be taken in the collection, analysis, and the interpretation of qualitative data.

References

American School Counselor Association. (2012). *The ASCA national model: A framework for school counseling programs* (3rd ed.). Alexandria, VA: Author.

Anderson, G. (1998). *Fundamentals of educational research* (2nd ed.). London: The Falmer Press.

Bloor, M., Frankland, J., Thomas, M., & Robson, K., (2001). *Focus groups in social research*. Thousand Oaks, CA: Sage.

Braun, V. & Clarke, V. (2006). Using thematic analysis in psychology. *Qualitative Research in Psychology*, 3, 77–101.

Centers for Disease Control and Prevention. (2010). *Practical strategies for culturally competent evaluation*. Atlanta, GA: US Department of Health and Human Services.

Denscombe, M. (2007). *The good research guide. For small-scale research projects* (3rd ed.). New York, NY: Open University Press.

Frierson, H. T., Hood, S., & Hughes, G. B. (2010) A guide to conducting culturally responsive evaluations. In J. Frechtling (Ed.), *The 2010 user-friendly handbook for project evaluation* (pp. 75–93). Washington, DC: National Science Foundation.

Glaser, B. G. & Strauss, A. L. (1967). *The discovery of grounded theory strategies for qualitative research*. New York: Aldine De Gruyter.

Guba, E. G. (1981) Criteria for assessing the trustworthiness of naturalistic inquiries. *Educational Communication and Technology Journal*, 29, 75–91.

Krueger, R. & Casey, M. A. (2000). *Focus groups: a practical guide for applied research* (3rd ed.). London: Sage.

Maguire, M. & Delahunt, B. (2017). Doing a thematic analysis: A practical, step-by-step guide for learning and teaching scholars. *All Ireland Journal of Teaching and Learning in Higher Education*, 8, 1–14.

Patton, M. Q. (2015). *Qualitative research and evaluation methods* (4th ed). Thousand Oaks, CA: Sage.

Public Policy Associates. (2015). *Considerations for conducting evaluation using a culturally responsive/racial equity lens*. Lansing, MI: Author.

Rallis, S. F. & Rossman, G. B. (2017). *An introduction to qualitative research* (4th ed.). Thousand Oaks, CA: Sage.

Shenton, A. K. (2004). Strategies for ensuring trustworthiness in qualitative research projects. *Education for Information*, 22, 63–75.

Smith, J. A., Flowers, P., & Larkin, M. (2009). *Interpretative phenomenological analysis: Theory, method and research*. London: Sage.

9 Reporting Evaluation Results and Using Findings

Questions to Consider

- What is the rationale for evaluation use?
- What are the types of evaluation use available to school counselors?
- What types of evaluation use fit best with your situation and work context? Why?
- What types of communication and reporting strategies would you use to foster use in your school?
- Consider an evaluation that you have knowledge of in your career. Was use fostered? If so, how?
- What type of technology-based communication methods do you have solid skill with? How would you use them to report evaluation findings?
- What are ways to foster use among culturally diverse stakeholder groups?

Vignette

Fairmont is a large school district in a metropolitan city. More than half of the students in this racially mixed school district receive free and reduced lunch, similar to other school districts within the city. There is a school counselor in all 14 school buildings, with two each for the three high schools. *Each school maintains an ASCA National Model program.* In addition, the school counselors work well together and maintain a district-wide school counseling focus as they work to maintain high-quality programming in each of their respective schools.

The school counseling program has embraced evaluation as a mechanism to build capacity, improve programs, and maintain accountability to school district stakeholders. **A key aspect of the evaluation work is on reporting and using the results.** *Evaluation is conducted every year. Each school generates an overall evaluation report* and a **district-wide evaluation report is also developed by a district administrator, with input from each school counselor. School counselors view these evaluation reports as a form of accountability, as these documents specify all aspects of the evaluation.** *These full evaluation reports are located on the school district website. In addition, annual presentations are made to the school board, school district administration, school community, and periodically to various community groups.*

The school counselors engage school counseling program stakeholders through development of evaluation questions. Evaluation reporting deliberately connects findings and recommendations to the agreed-upon evaluation questions. The transparency of this approach is appreciated by stakeholders and has, in part, increased broad support for the school counseling program throughout the school district. Moreover, school counselors conduct evaluation use meetings that are devoted to discussing the evaluation findings and recommendations, and consider ways to act on the findings. Outcomes from these meetings are further communicated to school, district, and community stakeholders through email and social media. In short, evaluation and subsequent reporting and use is integrated throughout each school counseling program within the district, and has become a routine part of the practice of school counselors.

Evaluation Reporting and Use is Fundamental

The aforementioned vignette depicts not only an ideal school counseling practice of conducting, reporting, and using evaluation information but also portrays what the ASCA National Model envisions for evaluation of school counseling programs. Referred to as Sharing Results, the ASCA National Model (ASCA, 2012) document states

> Regularly sharing results reports about the impact of the school counseling program with administrators, faculty and the school community in a document or in five- to 10-minute presentations will likely promote understanding, increase the value of and promote respect and indispensability for the work of professional school counselors (Dimmit, Carey, & Hatch, 2007; Young & Kaffenberger, 2009) (p. 104).

In addition, the ASCA National Model (ASCA, 2012) provides two recommendations for presenting the results of the evaluation that will help you convey balance and rigor to the stakeholder audiences present. In turn, stakeholders will more likely view the results as trustworthy. First, the ASCA National Model (ASCA, 2012) recommends that school counselors keep in mind that there are likely many variables explaining changes in student knowledge, attitudes, or behavior. The school counseling program intervention is one such variable. Thus, it is not a straightforward matter to make the argument that observed changes in students are directly and only attributed to the school counseling program itself. The ASCA National Model (ASCA, 2012) indicates that there is a difference between causation and correlation, and school counselors should convey this distinction to stakeholder audiences. The second recommendation is to focus solely on the contribution of the school counseling program to observed student changes, maintaining strong boundaries around what is under the purview and responsibility of school counselors and therefore, what is outside the scope of responsibility of school counselors.

The ASCA National Model document (ASCA, 2012) lists a variety of ways to communicate results. These include

- Websites
- One-page handouts
- Part of a larger report to administrators and school board members
- Presentation to faculty
- Part of the school's or district's data materials (p. 104)

This chapter expands on the above ASCA National Model recommendations and provides more detail and practical suggestions for maximizing the impact of evaluations through sharing and using results. The vignette in this chapter is illustrative of this idea by showing a school district that maintains strong ASCA National Model programs in each school. In addition to reporting to stakeholders as recommended, the school district incorporates stakeholders in the actual process of developing the evaluation through the evaluation questions. The school district connects findings to each evaluation question developed by stakeholders. This transparency helps stakeholders see the evaluation as credible, that their program needs and concerns are being addressed through the evaluation, which in turn, increases the likelihood of evaluation use.

Evaluation Standards that Support Reporting and Use

As the discipline and profession of evaluation has evolved, so has its awareness of the importance of evaluation reporting and use. In fact, Christie (2007) argued that evaluation use is viewed as so important to the field that it has become the most-researched construct in the evaluation literature. The JCSEE Program Evaluation Standards (Yarbrough et al., 2010) are clear about the expectation for evaluation reporting and use being a key aspect of the overall evaluation. Table 9.1 provides a sample of JCSEE Program Evaluation Standards from the utility and evaluation accountability attributes that attest to this idea (Yarbrough et al., 2010).

And of course, there are other standards that also point to the idea of effective evaluation reporting and use.

Based on the ASCA National Model document and the expectations from the evaluation profession, we promote the idea of school counselors conducting evaluations that are used to better the program, interventions, and services. And it is not just the school counselor that uses the evaluation findings. There are a broad set of users of school counseling evaluation that school counselors should be cognizant of and work toward meeting their information needs for evaluation use. Evaluations that foster use have the potential to pay dividends to the program by increasing knowledge and understanding about program

Table 9.1 Selected JCSEE program evaluation standards that support evaluation reporting and use

U7 Timely and Appropriate Communicating and Reporting	Evaluations should attend to the continuing information needs of their multiple audiences.
U8 Concern for Consequences and Influence	Evaluations should promote responsible and adaptive use while guarding against unintended negative consequences and misuse.
E1 Evaluation Documentation	Evaluations should fully document their negotiated purposes and implemented designs, procedures, data, and outcomes.

Source: From Yarbrough, D. B. et al. (2010). *The Program Evaluation Standards: A guide for evaluators and evaluation users* (3rd ed.). Thousand Oaks, CA: Corwin Press. Reproduced with permission from the Joint Committee for Standards in Educational Evaluation.

effectiveness to stakeholders, building and broadening support, and developing ways to provide the best program and services possible to serve the needs of students, teachers, and community members.

Types of Evaluation Use

Given the work in the evaluation field to better understand and promote evaluation use, some writers have developed frameworks and definitions of evaluation use. Besides the notion that evaluation use is, in the end, the main goal of doing evaluation, this work has also made clear that evaluation use is a multifaceted concept with different types of users and use. Be alert to the types of users and use that are articulated here and strategically consider when a particular type of use (for a particular user) could be beneficial. This is all part of the challenge of doing good evaluation work.

Mayne (2014) offers five ways in which evaluations can be used: (1) instrumental use, (2) conceptual use, (3) persuasive use, (4) process use, and (5) symbolic use. Each is briefly described and illustrated with examples from school counseling. Instrumental use is likely the most common idea people have about evaluation use. Evaluations provide recommendations. Acting on these recommendation(s) is instrumental use. Suppose a formative evaluation of your school counseling program was conducted. Suppose further that a recommendation was made to move the time a bullying prevention program that you were offering from the afternoon to the morning, to diminish the number of conflicts with academic coursework taught by teachers in the school. Moving the bullying prevention program to the morning is instrumental use of the evaluation.

Conceptual use refers to individual stakeholders learning more about a program through the evaluation. It could also refer to the idea of an individual considering other ways to think about the program. This type of use is connected to capacity building, as individuals build their knowledge and understanding about a program through the evaluation. Continuing with the bullying prevention program evaluation example, perhaps the evaluation stimulates stakeholders to consider other types of bullying prevention programs or ways to think about what the broader impact(s) could be from a bullying prevention program. Thus, conceptual use of the evaluation helps stakeholders consider the program in deeper and more-refined ways.

Conceptual use can benefit the program by expanding the number of individual stakeholders who know about the program in detail and can then productively advocate or promote the program or can think flexibly about proposed program changes. Legislators or school board members who know more about the inner workings of the bullying prevention program, and possibilities for positive outcomes, may be more likely to consider funding for the program, even during a time of budgetary constraints.

Using the evaluation to build support for or against a program is referred to as persuasive use. Suppose the yearly evaluation of the bullying prevention program offered in middle school showed that students who participate in the program are much less likely to participate or instigate acts of bullying. This information could be used to build further support for expanded implementation of the bullying prevention program.

When program personnel or stakeholders use the evaluation to build organizational learning, this is referred to as process use. School counselors in a school district that collectively discuss and react to the evaluation results of the bullying prevention program, is an example of process use. Considering the findings is a way for the school counseling team to build their collective knowledge and understanding of bullying prevention, particularly as it pertains to the program implemented within their schools and ways to enhance the delivery of the bullying prevention curriculum. Considering the evaluation as a group, school counselors could also build their knowledge and understanding of evaluation, all through the process of discussing the evaluation.

Symbolic use refers to using the evaluation for political reasons such as justifying previously made decisions. A superintendent wanting further political justification for a large district expenditure to obtain the bullying prevention program, could use evaluation findings to provide support for the expenditure to the school board, for example, as they review school district budgets.

As I think you'll infer, there is more to evaluation use than the logical and sometimes obvious instrumental use of the results. And not all uses of evaluation are positive in tone or outcome. Symbolic use for example, can be done to justify a program elimination decision, a decision that was made prior to the implementation of an evaluation. Of course, the evaluation is implemented with the idea that there would be enough negative findings that could be used to bolster the decision to eliminate the program. Most educators have had some experience with this type of evaluation use and, unfortunately, may have developed an uneasy concept of evaluation.

The point here is to make explicit the different types of evaluation use and to encourage you as a school counselor, to connect communication strategies and reporting formats effectively to foster a particular kind of use. This will

Table 9.2 Types of evaluation use

Type	Brief definition
Instrumental Use	Acting directly on evaluation recommendations.
Conceptual Use	Re-imagining the program based on the evaluation.
Persuasive Use	Using the evaluation to persuade people about the benefits of the program.
Process Use	Learning about the program and/or evaluation through reading and/or discussion of the evaluation.
Symbolic Use	Using the evaluation to justify a decision about the program that was previously made.

help you make the most of the evaluation findings for positive ends. It will also help you stay clear of evaluation used for unclear reasons, enhancing your professional credibility among stakeholders. Table 9.2 provides the types of evaluation use.

Evaluation Reports and Communication Forums

As you progress toward reporting and communicating findings of your school counseling evaluation and hold meetings or forums to present and discuss the results, keep in mind that each report and/or meeting has attached to it a type of evaluation use that can be used to promote and improve the school counseling program. Use these reporting and communication ideas strategically to advantage your school counseling program. In addition, remember that anytime evaluation information is communicated, stakeholders will test the communication for transparency and accountability. Stakeholders who were involved in developing evaluation questions or other aspects of the evaluation will want to know, for example, whether or not their information needs are being addressed. Other stakeholders may want to know whether or not the communication is balanced, objective, and comprehensive, and that inferences and recommendations are appropriately drawn from the data. While all of these issues would be difficult to address in, say, a 30-minute or one-hour meeting, know that how you communicate about the evaluation will in part determine, for those hearing or reading the communication, whether or not the information has veracity and, therefore, whether or not they can trust the evaluation process and findings.

BOX 9.1

Any communication about evaluation of the school counseling program will be assessed for transparency and accountability by program stakeholders.

Evaluation Reports

Reporting evaluation findings is an essential aspect of motivating evaluation use. There are traditional approaches to reporting findings and innovative approaches that use technology, such as social media. All have strengths and limitations. The central aspect of using a type of report or means of reporting is to use it strategically to increase understanding among those who choose to read the report or view the reporting mechanism and prepare for use of the results. Recall that the ASCA National Model (ASCA, 2012) makes a fairly straightforward recommendation of periodically reporting evaluation results. We expand on this important recommendation and do so with an eye toward evaluation use.

The most conventional form of reporting is through the use of evaluation reports. Think of an evaluation as having a beginning, middle, and end, like any task. A report while the evaluation is ongoing (interim report) could be used to communicate how things are going, challenges the evaluation could be experiencing, results gathered thus far, and a host of other things important for understanding the evaluation. Generally, these reports are brief, 2–10 pages, and could include a review of next steps in the evaluation. The report is used to inform but could also be used to stimulate comments from stakeholders, including suggestions for revisions to the evaluation. We recommend capturing these suggestions and responding to each one of them in a final report. Some suggestions will make sense and seem reasonable. Others may not be feasible, given the time and resources available for the school counseling program evaluation. Be clear about the differences in recommendations and articulate this in the report and through other means of communication. Keep in mind that being responsive to stakeholder concerns is essential for the evaluation to be viewed as credible, a precursor to evaluation use.

The final report is yet another conventional means of reporting results. The final report typically contains all information about the evaluation, from conceptualization to implementation, data analysis, and findings and recommendations. Given the length of this report and the technical aspects contained in it, the report is likely not read by many stakeholders. Nevertheless, we strongly recommend a final report for all evaluations. It is a means of transparency and accountability for the evaluation process and findings. It can be referred to should anyone have specific questions about the evaluation.

The final report often contains an executive summary. The executive summary is usually 2–10 pages and contains a distillation of the final report. The executive summary can be used as another means of reporting to stakeholders and, given its shorter length, may be a document more widely read.

There is no agreed-upon structure for any type of evaluation report. We recommend using the school counseling evaluation framework as a starting point in developing a structure for any of the reports. Here is a sample report structure for a final report:

- Executive Summary
- Background

- Identification and Involvement of Stakeholders
- Logic Model
- Evaluation Questions
- Evaluation Methods and Design
- Data Analysis
- Findings and Recommendations
- Appendices

Of course, this is a guideline. Depending on your evaluation and context, you might choose to revise this structure.

BOX 9.2

Think of an evaluation as having a beginning, a middle, and an end.

PowerPoint presentations are yet another common means to present evaluation findings or other aspects of the evaluation. A wonderful aspect of PowerPoint is the capability of providing information with multiple features to the text on the slide, including graphics. When done well, this can increase long-term retention of the information. Unfortunately, the technological capability in PowerPoint allows the development of slides that are cluttered with detail and graphics that can be confusing. When the presenter creates and uses PowerPoints that are busy and cluttered, the audience is left to wonder whether they should pay attention to the individual speaking or read the slides and ignore the speaker. All of this undermines understanding and long-term retention.

The American Evaluation Association has maintained a multi-year initiative to improve presentations. These ideas and recommendations can be applied to any type of evaluation-oriented presentation. Referred to as the Potent Presentations Initiative (p2i), it is a set of web-pages attached to the American Evaluation Association website that is full of wonderful suggestions to improve your presentations. We recommend referring to this website whenever you are preparing a presentation, particularly a PowerPoint presentation. The link is https://www.eval.org/p2i. Here are a few recommendations for creating slides:

- 24-point font or higher
- 1 or 2 font types
- 5–6 lines of text per page
- Strategic use of graphics

In short, use the technology to increase understanding; keep it simple and avoid clutter.

In recent years, various aspects of evaluation, particularly results, have been communicated through a variety of technologies. Many of these technologies are free over the internet. These include dashboards, interactive web-pages, blogs, YouTube videos, and data visualization tools, to name just a few. A one-page handout provided to participants at a meeting or made available to the general public can also be an effective way to communicate results. You can find more tools along with detail for each by accessing the website https://www.betterevaluation.org/en/blog/communicating-findings. All of these tools could be used to communicate aspects of your evaluation. Keep in mind that the tool is not an end in itself. The tool should be strategically used to communicate an aspect of your school counseling evaluation to stakeholders, in a way that increases understanding, transparency, and evaluation use.

Reporting Qualitative and Quantitative Methods

As advocated in this book, school counseling program evaluations can employ both qualitative and quantitative methods to collect the kind of data needed to answer the evaluation questions. Qualitative methods used in school counseling program evaluation could include, for example, observation or video of prevention program operation, examination of archival records that detail responsive services, or open-ended and semi-structured interviews that ask stakeholders about the quality of services. Quantitative methods include, for example, the statistical analysis of school profile data, student behavioral issues, and student achievement test scores. There is broad agreement among scholars and evaluators that the collection and integration of qualitative and quantitative data generally provide a more comprehensive and valid picture of the program. Torres, Preskill, and Pointek (2005) provide several recommendations when working to integrate qualitative and quantitative methods into evaluation communication and reporting. Three recommendations that we think are important for reporting evaluation of school counseling programs are presented here. One, obtain the help of individuals knowledgeable and skilled with each type of data collection method. By seeking help, no type of data will be shortchanged, and presentation of both qualitative and quantitative data will more likely be supported and done well. This is important for the credibility of the findings and will increase the likelihood of evaluation use. Two, develop a framework that will guide the presentation of qualitative and quantitative data. The most obvious is to use the evaluation questions as the guide. The appropriate data are then presented that answer a particular evaluation question. Three, determine the type of data that will be most appealing to a particular stakeholder group or audience and determine whether this type of data should be presented first. The idea behind this recommendation is to gain the group's attention and hold their attention so that they will seriously consider the findings. The other data could then be presented to complement or bolster the first presentation of data.

Evaluation Communication Forums

Schools and school districts have conventional, routine meetings that can be used to communicate about the evaluation findings of the school counseling program. These include school counselor meetings, school staff meetings, school district administrator meetings, school board meetings, and parent-teacher organization meetings. Take advantage of this built-in organizational meeting structure to communicate widely and purposefully about the evaluation findings. Each meeting is discussed below with an eye toward identifying the type of evaluation use the communication is attempting to achieve.

Meetings with School Counselors

Meetings with all school counselors in the school district are typically conducted on a routine basis, often monthly. These meetings are used to discuss a variety of issues important to school counselors and could be used to brainstorm strategies for addressing problems of one kind or another. These meetings are real possibilities for discussing the results of an evaluation of the school counseling program, either an individual school program or the school district as a whole.

To get the most out of these meetings, work with school counseling meeting facilitators to get time in the meeting to discuss the evaluation findings. Perhaps more than one meeting will be needed. Make sure that key aspects of the report are discussed (e.g., recommendations), rather than the report as a whole. And make sure that school counselors have the report with sufficient time to read it, with a clear understanding of what the discussion will entail and the desired outcome.

Whether the evaluation was focused on formative or summative evaluation, discussions could and should occur among school counselors so that they have processed the results and understand the implications. With respect to type of evaluation use, and the meeting and stakeholder group involved (i.e., school counselors), we suggest that instrumental, conceptual, and or process use could all be possibilities. Work to frame the evaluation discussion outcomes to foster one or more of these types of use.

School Staff Meetings

School staff meetings typically occur on a monthly basis. The school principal is likely responsible for the meeting agenda. Work with the principal to obtain time in the meeting to discuss the results. Again, make sure that school staff have a copy of the evaluation report or document well ahead of the meeting so that they have sufficient time to read and formulate thoughts they might have about the findings. Productive discussion at the meeting is more likely as a result. Types of evaluation use that are likely with school staff meetings include conceptual and process use primarily, and persuasive and symbolic use secondarily.

District Administrator Meetings

School district administrator meetings is yet another routine, likely monthly meeting that can be used as a forum to communicate school counseling evaluation findings. These meetings include school building and district-wide administrators. The school district superintendent is likely responsible for the agenda. Work accordingly to obtain meeting time to discuss the evaluation findings and make sure all participants have the necessary material ahead of time with a clear idea of the outcome of the discussion. As this meeting maintains all key decision-makers in the school district, conceptual, persuasive, and symbolic use are likely evaluation use outcomes from this meeting. Reduced to its essentials, communication at this meeting should include how the evaluation was conducted, the findings, and how recommendations will be addressed. In short, as school counselors, use this time to showcase transparency and accountability, and a willingness to act on the results. This strategy will help to obtain and keep support from key school district decision-makers.

School Board Meetings

School board meetings also likely occur monthly and have elected community members to the board. Most all school district administrators attend this meeting. As with school district administrator meetings, transparency and accountability are central to communicating about the school counseling evaluation findings. Work with the superintendent's office or appropriate individual to obtain time to make your evaluation presentation at the school board meeting. Ensure that all participants have appropriate materials and know the outcomes for the evaluation communication and discussion. In addition, given that school district administrators participate in school board meetings, ensure that all know ahead of time that the school counseling program evaluation will be discussed and the desired outcomes from the discussion. Reach out to administrators with an overview of the presentation so that they have an opportunity to consider concerns they might have about the program evaluation before the meeting. Conceptual, persuasive, and symbolic use are primary evaluation uses in reporting to school boards.

BOX 9.3

Ensure that meeting participants have advance copies of materials beforehand so they have sufficient time to read them and are not surprised by what is presented in the meeting.

Parent–Teacher Organization Meetings

Parent–teacher organization (PTO) meetings occur monthly and may occur more regularly. Since PTOs are composed of parents/guardians from individual schools, evaluation findings that address ways to improve the school counseling program and services will likely be of most interest. Meeting preparation recommendations that were articulated earlier also apply to PTO

Table 9.3 Primary evaluation uses for different types of meetings

Type of meeting	Evaluation use				
	Instrumental use	Conceptual use	Persuasive use	Process use	Symbolic use
School counselors	√	√	√		
School staff		√		√	
District administrators		√	√		√
School board		√	√		√
PTO		√	√		√

meetings. Conceptual, persuasive, and symbolic use are primary evaluation uses in this forum.

Of course, there are other meeting forums that could be used to communicate about the school counseling evaluation findings. Schools and school districts often have community meetings for different purposes and could be used to communicate about the evaluation findings. One-on-one or small-group meetings could also be established with school personnel or community members. Conceptually, there is no limit to the meeting possibilities. Table 9.3 provides the kinds of evaluation use that each type of meeting is best suited. The assessment captured in the table is based on the primary evaluation use for the meeting. Depending on context, any meeting or forum could be used to foster or address any type of evaluation use.

Reporting Results, Using Findings, and Culturally Responsive Evaluation

Reaching stakeholders from different cultural groups with your school counseling evaluation so that they read and react to it is central to conducting effective evaluation. For this to occur, stakeholders must view the evaluation as credible, responsive to their needs and concerns, and culturally relevant. Three recommendations are offered. One, as discussed in Chapter 5, a strategy for fostering a culturally responsive evaluation is to obtain from each cultural group the precise evaluation questions they think are important. While precise evaluation questions may not be articulated, as a school counselor, listen to the intent of what is said and work to develop evaluation questions that represent their concerns. Once the evaluation is conducted, communicate to them the evaluation questions they posed and show how the evaluation answered these questions. Two, if cultural groups in your school speak a language other than English, acquire the services of an individual who can present the evaluation in their language. Three, if certain types of data are important for a particular cultural group, include these data upfront in the evaluation. Storytelling for example, is important to some indigenous groups in Australia, Canada, New Zealand, and the US. Thus, including this type of data and doing so early in the communication about the evaluation will help to report on evaluation in a sensitive and responsive manner.

Summary

Effectively reporting and communicating evaluation findings is central to fostering evaluation use. Understanding the different types of evaluation use that can be fostered, the kind of use different school counseling stakeholder groups would most likely employ, and choosing reporting and communication strategies that supports and motivates the stakeholder desired use is part of the professional art and craft of doing evaluation work. The number of available reporting tools, especially technology-based tools, continues to grow. Any one of these tools could be used effectively, given the context. And it is not the tool itself that embodies effective reporting and communication. It is how the tool is used. Thus, being thoughtful about how and why particular tools are to be used is important to fostering evaluation use. Incorporating both qualitative and quantitative data collection methods will help to provide a more comprehensive picture of the school counseling program, as well as add validity and credibility to the evaluation. Using the evaluation questions developed by various cultural stakeholder groups and connecting findings to these questions will help to ensure a culturally responsive evaluation, an evaluation that will foster evaluation use.

References

American School Counselor Association (2012). *The ASCA national model: A framework for school counseling programs* (3rd ed.). Alexandria, VA: Author.

Christie, C. A. (2007). Reported influence on decision makers' actions: An empirical examination. *American Journal of Evaluation*, 28(1), 8–25.

Dimmitt, C., Carey, J. C., & Hatch, T. (2007). *Evidence-based school counseling: Making a difference with data-driven practices.* Thousand Oaks, CA: Corwin Press.

Mayne, J. (2014). Issues in enhancing evaluation use. In M. L. Loud, & J. Mayne (Eds.), *Enhancing evaluation use: Insights from internal evaluation units* (pp. 1–14). Thousand Oaks, CA: Sage.

Torres, R. T., Preskill, H., & Piontek, M. E. (2005). *Evaluation strategies for communicating and reporting* (2nd ed.). Thousand Oaks, CA: Sage.

Yarbrough, D. B., Shulha, L. M., Hopson, R. K., & Caruthers, F. A. (2010). *The program evaluation standards: A guide for evaluators and evaluation users* (3rd ed.). Thousand Oaks, CA: Corwin Press.

Young, A. & Kaffenberger, C. (2009). *Making data work* (2nd ed.). Alexandria, VA: American School Counselor Association.

10 Evaluation Knowledge Skills and Practice

Questions to Consider

- What knowledge and skills do I already have in evaluating the counseling program and its services?
- What knowledge and skills do I need to acquire in order to evaluate the counseling program and its services?
- How can I acquire the needed knowledge and skills?
- How do I decide how often and how much to evaluate?
- How can I work most effectively with school and district leaders regarding evaluation?
- How will I know when I need to engage an external evaluator?
- What should I look for in an external evaluator?
- What should I expect from an external evaluator?

Critical Program Evaluation Knowledge and Skills

Despite the fact that it is widely recognized that school counselors need to have competence in evaluation, a comprehensive list of essential competencies has not yet been developed. This lack of professional consensus on necessary evaluation competencies hampers the teaching of evaluation (Kose, 2019) and the assessment of new practitioners' competence in evaluation (Carey, Martin, Harrington, & Trevisan, 2019). A clear consensus on necessary competencies would also be very useful to practicing school counselors as they plan their professional development in program evaluation.

Kose (2019) has recently reviewed the literature on general program evaluation competencies and on school counselor program evaluation competencies. She concluded that current statements on school counselor competence focus on technical competencies (creating surveys, analyzing data, reporting results) but neglect other essential areas of competence, "such as managing interpersonal relationships, having the political savvy to navigate power structures in schools, understanding the interests of others, project management, or identifying and resolving ethical issues related to the evaluation" (p. 42).

Kose (2018) has proposed that school counselors' evaluation competencies can be organized in three interrelated domains: field-specific competencies, technical program evaluation competencies, and nontechnical program evaluation competencies. Field-specific competencies refer to the knowledge and skills necessary to develop, implement, and manage a comprehensive developmental school counseling program such as that described in the ASCA National Model (ASCA, 2012). Technical program evaluation competencies include knowledge of program evaluation concepts, theories, and goals; the skills associated with planning and conducting a competent, culturally responsive evaluation; and disseminating its results. Nontechnical evaluation competencies include the interpersonal skills needed to collaborate with stakeholders; manage the political aspects of the evaluation process; and anticipate, recognize, and resolve ethical issues in the evaluation process. The next three sections elaborate on these three domains to help you assess your current competence in program evaluation and plan your future learning.

BOX 10.1

It's important to self-assess your competence in program evaluation in order to plan your future learning.

Field Specific Competencies

A thorough knowledge of how to develop, implement, and monitor a comprehensive developmental school counseling program is a necessary foundation for effective evaluation. In addition, the ability to use the management and evaluation tools included in the ASCA National Model is essential. Table 10.1 contains a list of these field specific competencies that you can use to assess your current level of expertise.

These competencies can be developed through a university course dealing with the organization and administration of school counseling programs and through professional development study available through state and national professional associations.

Technical Program Evaluation Competencies

In addition to the basic competencies noted above, technical program evaluation competencies are also necessary. These competencies are related to the philosophy, concepts, and processes associated with the discipline of program evaluation as reflected in the school counseling evaluation framework presented in this book. Table 10.2 contains a list of these technical evaluation competencies that you can use to assess your current level of expertise.

These competencies can be developed through university courses in program evaluation or in university courses in research methods and statistics that have a

Table 10.1 Checklist of field specific competencies

Number	Competency
FS1	I understand the philosophy, principles, and structures of comprehensive developmental school counseling.
FS2	I can use the ASCA National Model *Foundation* tools to design a comprehensive developmental school counseling program.
FS3	I can conduct a *School Counseling Program Assessment* to determine the extent to which the elements of the ASCA National Model are present in the school counseling program.
FS4	I can conduct a *Use-of-Time Assessment* to assess how much time is spent on each of the four categories of service delivery.
FS5	I can conduct a yearly *Program Goals Assessment* to determine whether the goals for the counseling program are being met and whether program improvements are being implemented.
FS6	I can create a *School Data Profile* that includes all the important student achievement measures obtainable from school data so that these data can be used to identify problems that require the attention of school counselors.
FS7	I can develop *Action Plans* to guide implementation and evaluation for specific interventions, activities, or services that are intended to address identified problems.
FS8	I can develop *Action Plan Reports* in order to share the results of the evaluation-related activities with stakeholders.

strong evaluation component and orientation. Professional development study is also frequently available through state and national professional associations. We also recommend that working practitioners consider assembling an independent study group organized around this book.

Nontechnical Program Evaluation Competencies

Nontechnical competencies are also necessary for program evaluation. Program evaluation is not "values neutral." Evaluation always involves decision-making in complex social settings with multiple stakeholders who have differing needs, values, and perspectives. Stakeholders differ in the amount of decision-making power they have in the system. Often the intended beneficiaries of the program have the least amount of power to make important decisions about what services are delivered and how they are delivered.

In schools, a proper program evaluation requires the collection and analysis of sensitive information and the use of this analysis to improve services. This must be done in an ethical manner with respect for the stakeholders' rights to confidentiality.

To further complicate matters, school counselors engaged in evaluation are evaluating their own work and then sharing the results of this evaluation with their supervisors (and their supervisors' supervisors). This situation can create pressure to skew the evaluation methods and analyses to increase the likelihood

Table 10.2 Checklist of technical evaluation competencies

Number	Competency
TE1	I understand the goals of program evaluation and how it can be used to both improve services and demonstrate effectiveness and accountability.
TE2	I understand the differences between formative and summative evaluation.
TE3	I can identify the stakeholders of my program.
TE4	I can involve stakeholders in decisions about program design, evaluation, and improvement.
TE5	I can construct a logic model for my school counseling program.
TE6	I can construct a logic model for specific interventions, activities, and services.
TE7	I can use logic models to formulate formative and summative evaluation questions.
TE8	I can select strong quantitative, qualitative, and mixed-methods designs to address specific evaluation questions.
TE9	I can select and develop good instruments for collecting quantitative data.
TE10	I can select and develop good instruments for collecting qualitative data.
TE11	I can collect quantitative evaluation data in a variety of ways (e.g., closed-ended surveys, tests, school records).
TE12	I can collect qualitative evaluation data in a variety of ways (e.g., open-ended surveys, structured interviews, focus groups).
TE13	I can use basic statistical tests (t-tests and chi-square tests) to analyze change over time and group differences.
TE14	I can use rigorous qualitative procedures to identify perceptions and themes.
TE15	I can communicate evaluation results to stakeholders in a variety of formats and forums.
TE16	I can communicate evaluation results and work with stakeholders in a variety of ways to foster different types of evaluation use.
TE17	I can recognize when more advanced approaches to program evaluation are needed and can consult with external experts on evaluation design and data analysis.

that "positive" results will be found; that is, results that serve to confirm beliefs that current practice is maximally impactful and effective rather than results that can be used to improve current practice.

All these factors underscore the necessity of having competencies unrelated to professional and technical skills that are essential for effective evaluation. Table 10.3 contains a list of these nontechnical evaluation competencies that you can use to assess your current level of expertise.

The nontechnical evaluation competencies are complex and need to be developed in a different way from the previous competencies. Fortunately for counselors, these competencies overlap a good deal with the socio-emotional sensitivities and the skillset that is needed for effective counseling practices in schools. Many school counselors simply need to apply the competencies they already have to the new domain of evaluation. That said, supervised experience

Table 10.3 Checklist of nontechnical evaluation competencies

Number	Competency
NT1	I know how to give voice to disenfranchised stakeholders in decisions about program design, evaluation, and improvement.
NT2	I know how to establish and maintain trust with stakeholders.
NT3	I know how to safeguard stakeholders' privacy and confidential information.
NT4	I know how to generate an evaluation plan that takes into account the interests and viewpoints of multiple stakeholders.
NT5	I can create a climate of trust that allows people to report honestly their experiences, beliefs, and perceptions.
NT6	I know how to negotiate within the school system for the resources, time, and access to people that is needed for an effective evaluation.
NT7	I can present potentially unwelcome results in an honest and helpful fashion.
NT8	I can resist the temptation to seek confirmation of the value of my work in order to be able to learn how to improve it.

in evaluation is a very effective way to develop nontechnical competence (Kose, 2018). In the absence of this opportunity, we suggest that school counselors consult with peers during the course of an evaluation to identify evaluation issues that call for "soft skill" solutions and to brainstorm possible approaches.

Manageability: When, How Often, and How Much to Evaluate

This book builds on the evaluation expectations of the ASCA National Model. We think it provides the tools and framework to move evaluation from an ASCA National Model expectation and requirement to a vital set of ongoing functions that provide support and a sustainable platform for your school counseling program. With stakeholder involvement in one or more aspects of the evaluation process and informed by the standards of the evaluation field, the potential is high for evaluation to be a useful professional undertaking for school counselors that serves well the students, teachers, and families in the school.

We think the ASCA National Model evaluation expectations and this book complement one another. Together they provide you as a school counselor with the tools to conduct evaluation of your program with thoughtfulness, rigor, and transparency. Fulfilling the ASCA National Model expectations and conducting supportive evaluation through the school counseling evaluation framework contained in this book could position the school counseling program as the model for all other school and district programs regarding evaluation.

We offer the following guidelines to integrate ASCA National Model evaluation expectations with the school counseling evaluation framework and do so with the intent of making the program evaluation task manageable for a busy school counselor. Further, we hope to simplify the evaluation demands and put the enterprise in the hands of the professional school counselor.

First, make sure all the ASCA National Model tasks are completed as required. With this book, we are not suggesting that any of these tasks be eliminated. On the contrary, the ASCA National Model forms the basis of the school counseling program and provides professional recognition for the program and services you provide. Thus, all tasks are absolutely essential.

Two, while there are two main purposes for evaluation, program improvement, and program impact, we suggest that school counselors focus on evaluation for program improvement or formative evaluation. Formative evaluation has the potential to enhance day-to-day program operation, increase program potency to generate positive student outcomes, and maintain satisfied stakeholders, particularly those closest to the program.

Note that program impact is dealt with through the ASCA National Model tasks, such as *Curriculum Results Report* and the *Small-Group Results Report* (ASCA, 2012). Thus, summative evaluation also remains important for the school counselor. We are not suggesting that school counselors avoid summative evaluation. We are saying that from an evaluation point of view, one that is by definition constrained by time and resources, put your energies into formative evaluation. And when this occurs, summative evaluation, in whatever form, will more likely show the kind of impact outside stakeholders are most interested in.

Three, look for ways that the ASCA National Model expectations dovetail with the school counseling evaluation framework in this book and integrate the two. As an example, a feature of the *Curriculum Results Report* is that there is some focus on the extent to which the curriculum is implemented as planned and whether or not all students received the curriculum. These features signal formative evaluation for the purpose of program improvement and could be integrated into the school counseling evaluation framework in a straightforward manner. Other ASCA National Model expectations could be dealt with in a similar way.

Fourth, develop a multi-year evaluation plan and incorporate this plan into the calendar. Aspects could also be integrated into the various action plans required by the ASCA National Model. Share this calendar widely and post it in a public way, such as the school website.

In this way, you benefit by exercising control over the various evaluation tasks and activities by specifying when they will take place. The calendar allows you to spread the various aspects of the evaluation across the timeline so that they don't all happen at once. Further, the calendar provides a mechanism for all to see the various aspects of the evaluation and when they will occur, thus providing a measure of transparency and accountability. For those situations where there are too many evaluation questions to reasonably address, a multi-year timeline could afford you the opportunity to address some evaluation questions one year and others in a subsequent year, perhaps addressing all evaluation questions over time.

Fifth, as a means to lighten the load, the idea of incorporating stakeholders as expressed in this book could be a means of dividing the tasks and spreading

Table 10.4 Guidelines for managing the evaluation

Number	Guideline
1	Make sure all ASCA National Model evaluation tasks are fulfilled.
2	Focus your evaluation work on program improvement.
3	Look for ways the ASCA National Model expectations dovetail with the evaluation framework.
4	Develop a multi-year evaluation plan.
5	Involve stakeholders to lighten the workload.
6	Ask for additional resources.

the demands across more people. Of course, a good deal of work will be needed to think through how stakeholders could be involved and what kind of preparation they'll need. Refer back to Chapter 3 to refresh your thinking about use of stakeholders in the evaluation. There could be real payoff by including stakeholders to help with the evaluation workload.

Six, ask the building principal for additional resources. This could be in the form of budgetary resources, release time, or evaluation consultant help. All of these ideas could help you develop and implement your evaluation plan. And, asking school administrators for additional help is your prerogative. The aforementioned guidelines are summarized in Table 10.4.

Evaluation in the School Organizational Context

Whether you are in a small rural school district or a large suburban or urban school district, there is an organizational structure and it can sometimes be complicated to navigate. As a school counselor, you have or you will develop a sense of what works for you and your program in navigating the system.

Recall from Chapter 3 that there are a variety of school and district stakeholders that likely have expectations about the school counseling program and its evaluation. Keeping these ideas in mind as you move forward will continue to be important. To be sure, some of these stakeholders are administrators. Key among them are the school principal, the school district coordinator or director for the school counseling program, and the superintendent. Close communication with each of them is important to keep them informed of your program and evaluation. Personal meetings, email, and phone could all be communication mechanisms you use to discuss any issues or important features of the school counseling program and evaluation. How much to communicate, how frequently, and in what way will differ from school district to school district. By being forthright, you are taking control of some of the nontechnical aspects of addressing the evaluation with important stakeholders and decision-makers. Find what works in your situation and stay with it. You are the best spokesperson for the school counseling program and evaluation.

Administration inevitably changes in schools and school districts, and thus, different leadership could demand changes to structures, processes, and priorities. If a change in principal is to occur, seek ways to communicate with the current principal and incoming principal about the importance of the school counseling program. With a good relationship with the current principal, express your concern for communicating about the school counseling program with the new principal. The current principal may want to do this at the administrative level. Make sure your current principal has a recent copy of the program evaluation and encourage her or him to provide this to the incoming principal. The same strategy could be used when changes in other administrative positions occur. Remember that the recent evaluation report signals transparency and accountability for the school counseling program. Recent copies of the report should be part of the communication that takes place in whatever administrative change that occurs.

Larger school districts may take a more centralized view of the school counseling programs and services. As a consequence, there could be an expectation for district-wide evaluation of the school counseling programs. While this might make sense conceptually, it can seem redundant given the ASCA National Model (ASCA, 2012) expectation for school-level program evaluation.

District-wide evaluation will likely focus on impact and, thus, summative evaluation. In addition, it's likely that the school district evaluation specialist (assuming there is someone in a position like this) will perform the evaluation, or an evaluator external to the school district could be hired on contract to perform the evaluation.

Should this be the case, this book provides the content and recommendations to help you work productively within the district-wide evaluation and organizational context. As a school counselor and key stakeholder, ask questions about the evaluation and process if this is not clear to you. Offer to be part of developing evaluation questions. Ask for progress and final evaluation reports. In short, all the recommendations made earlier in this book for working effectively with stakeholders, including communication and reporting, apply now for you as a stakeholder. Use these recommendations to your advantage to advocate for sound, balanced, and transparent evaluation of the school district's school counseling programs and services. Nothing less is acceptable. In short, the evaluator and school district administration must also be accountable. Everyone wins when this occurs, particularly the school counseling program and the students it serves.

BOX 10.2

In order to have maximal impact, it is important to consider the context of your school and school district as you plan and implement an evaluation.

Working with an External Evaluator

While it is important for all school counselors to be able to conduct program evaluation, it is sometimes necessary to work with an external evaluator. An external evaluator will be necessary when the program evaluation is complex and/or requires advanced expertise in evaluation design and data analyses. School counselors are needed in schools to counsel. For a complex whole program or whole district evaluation, it makes sense to engage with an evaluator who can share this work. Likewise, when evaluation questions require complex designs and statistical analyses, it is generally more efficient to work with an evaluator who already has this expertise.

Political considerations often mitigate toward the engagement of an external evaluator. If there is a lack of trust (among the school counselors, administrators, teachers, parents, and/or students), it may not be advisable for school counselors to be the exclusive evaluators of their own work since the results of the evaluation need to be trusted in order to be believed, accepted, and acted upon. In these instances, it may make good sense to engage an external evaluator who will be perceived as more unbiased and credible.

In selecting an external evaluator, it is important to consider how much experience the evaluator has with school-based programs (preferably comprehensive developmental school counseling programs). It is important to consider how their technical evaluation competencies match with the type of evaluation that is required. It is also essential to consider if they have the nontechnical competencies that will be necessary to design and conduct an evaluation in the complex social system of the school. The competencies contained in Tables 10.1, 10.2, and 10.3 are a useful list of criteria for a highly competent external evaluator. In the selection of an external evaluator, it is also helpful to consider the extent to which they understand and adhere to the JCSEE Program Evaluation Standards (Yarbrough et al., 2010).

We strongly recommend choosing a professional evaluator who understands the field of program evaluation, has experience with school-based programs and multiple stakeholders, is committed to the highest professional standards for evaluation, has the necessary technical skills, and has the nontechnical skills to conduct an effective evaluation in a complex social milieu. Many people are selling their supposed evaluation expertise, and it is important not to hire a survey developer when you need an evaluator!

Welcome to "The Club"

Welcome to the end of this book and the beginning of your journey. Having successfully navigated your way through this book, you are ready to begin your work in school counseling program evaluation. Admittedly, you and we all still have a lot to learn about evaluating and improving programs. When you bump into something that you still need to learn, please do not let it distract you from appreciating how much you already know, how much you have already learned, and how much good you have already done. Evaluation is a complex act requiring both technical skill and social intelligence. It gets better with experience, reflection, and dialogue. Talk about your evaluation work with your colleagues. Ask them about their evaluation work. Share your successes and failures. Both are educative. Both talking and listening will help you grow in your ability to ensure that all the children and youth who are under your care get the quality of attention and service that they deserve. You can let yourself feel justifiably proud about that. We can also let ourselves feel justifiably proud if we have helped you to get there.

References

American School Counselor Association. (2012). *The ASCA national model: A framework for school counseling programs* (3rd ed.). Alexandria, VA: Author.

Carey, J. C., Martin, I., Harrington, K., & Trevisan, M. S., (2019). Competence in program evaluation and research assessed by state school counselor licensure examinations. *Professional School Counseling, 22*, 1–11.

Kose, A, (2018). Program evaluation competencies and training for prospective school counseling practitioners. Unpublished manuscript.

Kose, A. (2019). Program evaluation competencies for prospective school counseling practitioners. *International Journal of Curriculum and Instructional Studies, 9*(1), 33–52.

Yarbrough, D. B., Shulha, L. M., Hopson, R. K., & Caruthers, F. A. (2010). *The Program Evaluation Standards: A guide for evaluators and evaluation users* (3rd ed.). Thousand Oaks, CA: Corwin Press.

Glossary

Accountability The process of showing publicly the extent to which taxpayer money was spent wisely and that intended outcomes were achieved. Accountability is usually associated with summative evaluation, which is often conducted by an external evaluator. However, formative evaluation conducted by school counselors, for example, can also be viewed as a form of accountability, particularly when the evaluation is implemented in a transparent manner and reported publicly.

Action plans ASCA National Model practices that support the planning, implementation, and evaluation of specific interventions and activities of the program including "curriculum" (preventative classroom-based lessons), "small groups," and "closing-the-gap." Action plans include a description of goals, procedures, and evaluation methods.

Activities in a logic model Activities are the components of a program that are intended to result in learning and behavior change and consequently are responsible for creating benefits for program participants. School counseling program activities include both direct (e.g., group counseling) and indirect services (e.g., teacher consultation). See also **logic model**.

Advisory council An advisory council is a representative group of stakeholders that advises on the implementation of the school counseling program. The advisory council is a necessary component of the ASCA National Model. Meetings are typically held twice per year. A chairperson is elected, terms for membership established, and meeting agendas and minutes are established and recorded.

Alpha error Common error in judgments about program impact based on statistical analysis of quantitative evaluation data where a difference is mistakenly judged to be real when in fact it is due to chance variation. For example, with a significance level set at .10, an alpha error will occur 10% of the time. See also **alpha level**.

Alpha level The decision point made by the school counselor in order to make the claim that because the probability of an observed difference is so low, the difference is more likely to be due to the program intervention. The traditional alpha level in research is .05. A common alpha level in program evaluation is .10. In order to make the claim of program impact (statistical significance), the observed difference, once subjected to a statistical test, must have a probability of .10 or less. The alpha level is established prior to computing the statistical test. The alpha level, sometimes referred to as significance level, also signals alpha error, the probability of claiming that a program has had an impact when in fact the difference found is simply due to chance. See also **alpha error**.

ASCA National Model   A comprehensive developmental school counseling program that focuses on enhancing students' academic achievement and that includes the foundation, management, delivery system, and accountability practices endorsed by the American School Counselor Association (ASCA, 2012).

Beta error   Common error in judgments based on statistical analysis of quantitative evaluation data. The error in judgement occurs when a real difference is mistakenly judged to be due to chance variation.

Capacity building   Capacity building refers to the development of professional knowledge and skills, expanding the types of tasks and activities or capacity of an individual. With respect to including stakeholders in the development of evaluation questions, the activity can expand the capacity of stakeholders to understand and participate in the evaluation.

Case study evaluation designs   Category of qualitative evaluation designs that involve the in-depth, holistic investigation of single individuals, programs, or policies in order to describe or explain them. Case studies typically involve the collection and integration of qualitative data from multiple sources (e.g., records, interviews, observations) in order to understand the operation of a program. See also **qualitative evaluation designs**.

Chi-square test   Statistical test used to determine the likelihood that an observed difference between two or more groups is due to chance variation. Best used with nominal level data.

Closed-ended survey questions   Survey questions where respondents choose their response from among a fixed set of pre-established alternatives. Closed-ended surveys are typically used in obtaining quantitative data for evaluations.

Comprehensive developmental school counseling program   A component of a school with its own curriculum, management practices, and program evaluation practices that focuses on the delivery of a variety of interventions and activities to promote the cognitive, personal/social, and career development of students.

Conceptual use   Conceptual use occurs when individuals read or hear about an evaluation and learn more about the program itself, other types of similar programs, and what could be possible within the boundaries of the various versions of the program. See also **evaluation use**.

Culturally responsive evaluation   Program evaluation that specifically addresses and responds to the cultural aspects of a program. Culturally responsive evaluation is evaluation that is done with cultural competence.

Culturally responsive evaluation is not merely a list of expectations that should be followed. Rather, it is a stance one takes in acknowledging that culture plays a part in a particular program and, therefore, the evaluation. Culturally responsive evaluation is an ethical imperative for the American Evaluation Association and a matter of validity for evaluation findings.

Data-based decision-making   Data-based decision-making (DBDM) can be defined as "the process of collecting, analyzing, reporting and using data for school improvement" (Dahlkemper, 2002, p. 1). DBDM largely relies on the use of existing school data to define foci for school improvement activities and on comparatively simple analytic procedures for judging the success of these activities.

Distal outcomes in a logic model   Distal outcomes are the expected long-term benefits of program participation. See also **logic model**.

Ethnographic evaluation designs   Category of qualitative evaluation designs that involve the investigation of human interactions within a defined setting. Originally developed in the field of anthropology, ethnographic designs are particularly useful in identifying the unspoken rules of program operation that govern interactions and that affect the availability, quality, equity, and access of program services. See also **qualitative evaluation designs**.

Evaluation communication forums   Face-to-face meetings to discuss aspects of a program evaluation are referred to as evaluation communication forums. Examples include staff meetings, community meetings, school board meetings, school-parent meetings, and one-on-one meetings.

Evaluation framework   A six-component model used to guide the development and implementation of the evaluation of a school counseling program. The six components are (1) stakeholder involvement, (2) theory of action, (3) evaluation questions, (4) evaluation design and method, (5) data analysis and findings, and (6) evaluation reporting and use.

Evaluation plan   A plan that includes a description of which data will be collected and how these data will be analyzed to answer each of the evaluation questions.

Evaluation question   Evaluation questions provide direction and focus to a program evaluation. Evaluation questions work to provide answers to questions about program effectiveness and efficiency and program impact. Specifically, a central formative evaluation question is, "Is the program working well?" A central summative evaluation question is, "What is the impact of the program?" The next step in the evaluation would then be to establish an evaluation strategy that would answer the questions so that sound decision-making about the program can occur.

Evaluation use   The process of using evaluation results and recommendations to enhance learning and or decision-making. Sometimes referred to as utilization, evaluation use is the main goal of any evaluation.

Focus groups   Qualitative method of collecting evaluation data where the evaluator brings together a small group of people (typically 6–9) and moderates a discussion of predetermined topics aligned with the evaluation questions. A record of the discussion is analyzed using qualitative analytic procedures.

Formative evaluation   Evaluation used to obtain information about how well the program was implemented, what is working well, and what needs revision. Formative evaluation also seeks to determine how satisfied key stakeholders are with the program. Formative evaluation is typically focused on the day-to-day operation of the program. In sum, formative evaluation provides information to improve the program.

Grounded theory evaluation designs   Category of qualitative evaluation designs that involve the systematic generation of a theory concerning a given phenomenon. It is based upon the analysis of qualitative data that are collected and analyzed in a standardized manner. Evaluators generate a theory that describes the operation of a program inductively through the coding of stakeholder interviews. See also **qualitative evaluation designs**.

Inputs in a logic model   Inputs include all the resources that are necessary for the effective delivery of the activities of the program. These include facilities, materials, and expertise. See also **logic model**.

Instrumental use   A type of evaluation use in which people act on recommendations made in the evaluation. This is typically what many people think about when they think of evaluation use. See also **evaluation use**.

Intended outcomes   Expressly desired impacts or accomplishments as a result of the program. For example, a bullying prevention program seeks to reduce bullying. The reduction of bullying is an intended outcome.

Interpretive phenomenological analysis   A well-accepted approach for identifying themes in the analysis of qualitative evaluation data which is best suited to in-depth interview data. See also **phenomenological evaluation methods**.

Lesson plan   ASCA National Model practice that supports the planning, implementation, and evaluation of classroom lessons delivered by school counselors. Lesson plans include a description of the learning objectives, instructional materials and procedures, and an evaluation plan. Evaluation results are distributed to school administration, stakeholders, and the school community.

Level of significance   Criterion used in statistical analysis to decide when an observed difference between groups can be judged to be real. Note that the significance level is also the alpha level. With an alpha set at .10, for example, only 10% of the time will differences that are judged to be real actually be due to chance variation. See also **alpha error**.

Levels of measurement   Different types of quantitative data that reflect the appropriate ways that the data can be summarized and analyzed. Quantitative data can represent a numerical name (nominal data), an ordinal position (ordinal data), or scores on a scale (interval or ratio data).

Logic model   A logic model is a graphic representation of a theory of action that includes all the essential components of the program and the hypothesized relationships among these components. The logic model is developed in order to identify evaluation questions.

Mixed-methods evaluation designs   Evaluation designs for the collection and analysis of both qualitative and quantitative data to answer evaluation questions.

Nominal data   Type of quantitative data where the numbers reflect counts related to group membership. Nominal data are best summarized by percentages and analyzed by nonparametric procedures like chi-square tests. See also **levels of measurement**.

Nonequivalent control group design   Quantitative evaluation design where data are collected and analyzed from treatment and comparison groups, before and after a program's activity. See also **quantitative evaluation designs**.

One-group pretest-posttest design   Quantitative evaluation design where data are collected and analyzed from one group, before and after a program's activity. See also **quantitative evaluation designs**.

Open-ended survey questions   Survey questions where respondents write their own responses according to their personal beliefs, attitudes, and feelings. Open-ended surveys are typically used in qualitative evaluations.

Ordinal data   Type of quantitative data where the numbers reflect ordinal position. With ordinal data, judgments need to be made about whether it is more appropriate to treat it like nominal data or scale data in summaries and analyses. See also **levels of measurement**.

Outputs in a logic model   Outputs are the changes in program participants that are expected to occur immediately after the activity. Outputs are also called "immediate outcomes." From an evaluation perspective, outputs can be thought of as the immediate evidence that the activity has had an effect. See also **logic model**.

Persuasive use   Using the evaluation to persuade others about the program. For example, using the evaluation to promote the benefits of a program is an example of persuasive use. See also **evaluation use**.

Phenomenological evaluation designs   Category of qualitative evaluation designs that involve describing and explaining a particular program or activity through the systematic collection and analysis of the beliefs, impressions, and judgments of people who have had experience with it. There are many specific methodologies for collecting, analyzing, and reporting phenomenological data. Phenomenological designs offer practical, flexible, powerful, and easy-to learn approaches to the formative and summative evaluation of the school counseling program. See also **qualitative evaluation designs**.

Phenomenological evaluation methods   Evaluation designs for the collection and analysis of qualitative data to answer evaluation questions.

Posttest–only control group design   Quantitative evaluation design where data are collected and analyzed from treatment and comparison groups, after a program's activity. See also **quantitative evaluation designs**.

Process use   When program personnel or stakeholders use the evaluation to build organizational learning, this is referred to as process use. See also **evaluation use**.

Program theory evaluation   Program theory evaluation is an approach to program evaluation that maps the logic underlying a program and its activities and tests whether or not desired results are being attained. Such an evaluation starts with the development of a theory of action that specifies the hypothesized relationships between resources, activities, and outcomes. The evaluation is then designed to test these hypotheses.

Proximal outcomes in a logic model   Proximal outcomes are the changes in program participants that are expected to be evident in the weeks and months after participation in a program activity. These reflect the demonstration of attitudes, knowledge, and behavior that increase the likelihood that long-term positive benefits will result. See also **logic model**.

Qualitative data   Evaluation data that cannot be adequately expressed as numerical quantities. Qualitative data reflect subjective descriptions that when properly analyzed, provide answers to evaluation questions.

Qualitative evaluation designs   Evaluation designs for the collection and analysis of qualitative data to answer evaluation questions.

Quantitative evaluation designs   Evaluation designs for the collection and analysis of quantitative data to answer evaluation questions.

Results reports   ASCA National Model practices that support the dissemination of program evaluation results to school administration, school community, and other stakeholders. Results reports are based on the specific interventions and activities of the program including "curriculum" (preventative classroom-based lessons), "small groups," and "closing-the-gap" that are planned, implemented, and evaluated through action plans.

Scale data   Type of quantitative data where the numbers reflect qualities measured on psychometric scales. Scale data are best summarized by means (averages) and analyzed by parametric procedures like t-tests. See also **levels of measurement**.

School counseling program   Component of a school with its own goals, management practices, and program evaluation practices that focuses on the delivery of a variety of interventions and activities to promote the learning, development, and well-being of students.

School counseling program assessment   An ASCA National Model audit for the school counseling program to determine whether or not the essential elements of the ASCA National Model are being implemented.

School data profile   ASCA National Model feature where school counselors maintain a database that includes the essential student achievement-related measures obtainable from school data (e.g., attendance rates). These data are used for identifying needed interventions, activities, and services and for evaluating change after program delivery.

Stakeholder Any individual or group with some vested interest in the school counseling program. This could include students, parents, teachers, school principal, district administration, community members, and taxpayers. Note that school counselors are also stakeholders in the program.

Stakeholder involvement Stakeholder involvement is the process of involving stakeholders in one or more aspects of the program evaluation. Involving stakeholders in developing evaluation questions is crucial, as the evaluation questions reflect what is important to stakeholders and drive the program evaluation. Involving stakeholders could require professional development because some stakeholders may not have the evaluation background necessary for the work.

Standards The JSCEE Program Evaluation Standards (Yarbrough et al., 2010) are a set of 30 standards that signal high-quality evaluation. The 30 standards are divided into the following five categories or attributes: utility, feasibility, propriety, accuracy, and accountability. The JSCEE Program Evaluation Standards can be thought of as guidelines to be applied flexibly given the context of the evaluation.

Structured individual interviews Qualitative method of collecting evaluation data where the evaluator asks respondents to address individually a predetermined set of questions that are aligned with evaluation questions. Individual responses are analyzed using qualitative analytic procedures.

Summative evaluation Evaluation used for summing up the overall impact of the program. The focus of summative evaluation is to document whether or not intended outcomes have been obtained and to determine whether or not unintended consequences of the program occurred. Evaluation results from summative evaluation are typically used to provide policy makers and other decision-makers information that they can use to determine next steps for the program. Summative evaluation also provides a form of accountability.

Symbolic use Conducting an evaluation for political purposes, such as to justify or bolster a political decision that has already been made about a program, is symbolic use. See also **evaluation use**.

T-test Statistical test used to determine the likelihood that an observed difference between two groups is due to chance variation. Best used with scale level data.

Thematic content analysis A well-accepted, flexible, and adaptable approach for identifying themes in the analysis of a wide range of different types of qualitative evaluation data. See also **phenomenological evaluation methods**.

Theory of action A theory of action is a description of the logic underlying the operation of a program. It is an essential element of program theory evaluation. A theory of action is generated to ensure that all the *implicit* assumptions and beliefs about a program are made *explicit* so that they can be examined, verified, and evaluated. The theory of action guides the development of the evaluation plan.

Trustworthiness of qualitative evaluation findings   The degree to which the results of a qualitative evaluation can be relied upon to be accurate and truthful. According to Guba (1981), trustworthy findings are findings that are credible, dependable, confirmable, and transferable. Trustworthiness can be ensured by using established methods of qualitative data collection and analysis, the evaluator identifying their own beliefs and biases, triangulation of findings to verify their consistency, periodic debriefing with peers during the evaluation, and having stakeholders review the analyses and interpretations.

Unintended consequences   Outcomes or impacts that occurred as a result of the program but were not intended as part of the program. Unintended consequences could be positive or negative. They are usually identified as part of summative evaluation.

Use-of-time assessment   ASCA National Model practice that involves the documentation of the amount of counselor time spent on each of four categories of service delivery in order to determine if counselors are allocating efforts in ways that can be expected to support effective program implementation.

Index